Clinics in Developmental Medicine No. 54

A Neurobehavioural Study in Pre-School Children

by

ALEX FEDDE KALVERBOER

1975

Spastics International Medical Publications

LONDON: William Heinemann Medical Books Ltd.

PHILADELPHIA: J. B. Lippincott Co.

HH IM

ISBN O 433 18260 1

Printed in England at THE LAVENHAM PRESS LTD., Lavenham, Suffolk

To Minnie, Karin, Margrite and Alle Fedde

Contents

Acknowledgements

This study results from the co-operation between researchers of different disciplines in the Department of Developmental Neurology at Groningen University. The theme studied was the development of the central nervous system; around this theme each researcher worked on his own ideas and also contributed as a member of the group. The study was a unique form of interdisciplinary work in which the exchange of ideas was as important as the exchange of data.

Professor Heinz Prechtl's views on the structure and content of scientific work gave coherence to the study and led to a common problem-oriented approach. The planning, data collection, analysis and the writing up of the research were influenced greatly by the many inspiring discussions with him during crucial phases of the study.

Thanks are due also to Dr. Bert Touwen, who collected and analysed the neurological data, and without whose help this study would not have been possible.

Special thanks are due to Dr. John O'Brien; his critical, logical thinking and our many discussions helped greatly in improving the final shape of the report.

I am grateful also to Harmke Sanders and Mrs. van Dijk. They were of great assistance in helping with the observations, video recordings, and administration and recording of numerous psychological examinations.

Gré Kremer and Frouwkje Boonstra helped in making contact with the children's parents. It was due mainly to them that so many parents agreed to participate in the study.

Wim Koops and Mila Smrkovsky helped in the difficult task of analysing the enormous amounts of data; their contributions to decisions about data processing, as also their technical aid, were indispensable.

Many people outside the Department helped enormously. In this respect, I must thank Pieter Boeke for his valuable criticism and suggestions in the latter part of the study. Professor Ivo Molenaar assisted in assessing the manuscript and gave important advice on the statistical analyses and their presentation. Leo van der Weele helped in the computer analyses and programming of data.

Tineke Veenstra has typed and re-typed many versions of this manuscript and I thank her for her precision and unbelievable patience.

Leo van Eykern gave invaluable technical assistance and drew several of the illustrations.

Wiekie Lems has collaborated in the study in a variety of ways; in the planning, statistical calculations, drawing of graphs, correction of text and references, and many other activities, without which a study of this kind could not have been completed.

Dr. Martin Bax of Spastics International Medical Publications has been of great assistance in the preparation of the text for publication.

The photographs were taken by Mr. Hoks of the Department of Clinical Neurology, University Hospital, Groningen, and also by the Centrale Fotodienst of Groningen University.

Finally, I acknowledge my debt to the Department as a whole, for making it possible for me to finish this study and for protecting me—especially in the last stages of preparing the manuscript—from outside disturbances.

This work was supported by a grant from the Organisation for Health Research (T.N.O.), Netherlands.

Preface

The introduction of quantitative ethology into medicine in the early 1950s came about because there were then many epileptic children with the hyperkinetic syndrome. These children had survived brain insults formerly mortal, and were left with lesions in their limbic systems. Anticonvulsant medication released overactivity in them, and their hyperkinesis was such that no test could be applied to them. Those doctors brave enough to venture had their spectacles smashed, their forms torn up and their desks wrecked. All that one could do was to observe and to time the children's spontaneous behaviour. From this start, more sophisticated studies arose, to which the present book is a welcome addition.

The triumphs of ethology have led to much unwise extrapolation from other animals to our own species. We must constantly remember that we must 'know our own animal' if we are to be good human ethologists. The present work aims at just this. With painstaking care, data on the actual behaviour of children have been collected systematically and analysed. The results go far to end the dangerous concept of 'Minimal Brain Dysfunction' (M.B.D.) and the facile hypothesis of the 'Continuum of Reproductive Casualty'. These are two major achievements.

The author points out that the techniques of quantitative ethology have been given rigorous trials and that their application in fields such as neuropharmacology is now both possible and urgent.

Ethological techniques are difficult, especially for doctors. In medicine, it is now traditional to regard the patient as a subject; one who is subjected to a series of tests without exhibiting any of his own idiosyncratic repertoire of behaviour. For those interested in the brain and its development, quantitative ethology is the best, and indeed the only, way in which the actual workings of the untrammelled brain can be studied properly. Little or no experimentation is done in this science and this is why people find it hard to understand that this is scientific. It should be remembered that the first and most precise science was astronomy, and, in this, until very recently, experiments were never made. In the study of sex differences (on which the author presents fascinating analyses), tests commonly revealed no difference at all between boys and girls. But, as every mother knows, their patterns of behaviour do differ from the start and simple observation will show it.

Perhaps works such as the present one may not only advance our knowledge but also lead back to an older and healthier attitude to our patients. Let us find out what they really do.

Christopher Ounsted

Park Hospital for Children,
Oxford,
England.

CHAPTER 1

Introduction

The work reported in this book had two main aims. The first was to develop appropriate techniques for studying the behaviour of young children, and the second was to try and introduce some clarity into the discussions about the relationships between behaviour and neurological disorders in young children. Both these topics have been of continuing interest to the workers in the Department of Developmental Neurology at Groningen, and numerous previous studies of younger infants have gone far in standardising techniques of neurological examination (Prechtl and Beintema 1964, Touwen and Prechtl 1970) and also in developing sophisticated ways of looking at behavioural states, particularly in young infants (*e.g.* Prechtl 1968). The present study tackles the problem of recording the behaviour of older children and relating this to neurological findings.

The relationships between the older child's behaviour and performance in school and his neurological status have also attracted a great deal of attention in recent years, and have been the subject of studies not only in Groningen (Prechtl and Stemmer 1962) but also in many other centres of the world. The nebulous syndromes of 'minimal brain damage', 'minimal cerebral dysfunction' and a host of other names have led to the publication of a large amount of literature on the behaviour of minimally brain-damaged children, but very few of these studies, as I shall discuss in Chapter 7, contain much reliable information about the relationships between behaviour and the neurological status of the child. In particular, the statements made about children's behaviour have usually been rather subjective and some of the few worthwhile studies have served to demonstrate this subjectivity (Schulman *et al.* 1965, Rutter *et al.* 1970). But such subjectivity is inevitable, until reliable methods of measuring and recording behaviour are developed.

The present study, therefore, has clinical relevance in two ways. Although the procedure described is not directly applicable in the clinical situation, being too time-consuming, it does serve to emphasise the variations in behaviour that do occur with quite small changes in the environment, such as the removal of some toys from a room, and can give the clinician insight into the difficulties of assessing behaviour in an ordinary clinical setting. In addition, however, the methods of study we describe are important tools in clinical research and can be adapted to clinical settings; we are currently using these techniques in clinical studies of so-called autistic, and hearing-impaired children and in children who have had traumatic brain injury. At the moment such studies are inevitably rather expensive, but one of our purposes is to identify the most critical behaviours and environments for study and, in time, to produce a practical clinical tool.

A great deal of clinical data about children's behaviour is collected either by direct history taking or in the form of questionnaires. It is not surprising if these studies rarely show very consistent relationships between the neurological status of the child and reports of disturbed behaviour. It is much more likely that directly-observed behaviour will relate to neurological status, as the clinical neurological examination itself is in part a detailed observation of behaviour.

If one can relate closely-observed behaviour to the neurological status of the child, the next step is to see how far this behaviour correlates with the child's 'spontaneous' behaviour at home and at school and in any other environment in which he finds himself. Direct observation of such behaviour is, of course, difficult, and that is why, at present, we depend on historical accounts and questionnaires. The present study tries to narrow the gap between what the child actually does and the way others perceive him.

There are considerable difficulties in undertaking neurobehavioural studies. Most ideas about children's behaviour have, until very recently, been dominated by analytic psychiatry and psychology, where it was often felt that it was difficult to draw any inferences about the child's emotional status from observing him (for an interesting discussion of this see Bowlby (1971)). Starting work in this field, one finds oneself faced with an almost complete lack of normative data about children's behaviour and it is not easy to decide even when a reported behaviour should be regarded as pathological or as normal.

In the interpretation of neurological findings we are faced with similar problems. Age norms for the neurological repertoire of the child are still insufficient. In pre-school children, only a few data on the distribution of single neurological signs have been reported up till now (Connolly and Stratton 1968, Grant *et al.* 1973). Establishing such age norms is a very time-consuming and difficult procedure.

Particular care should be taken over the interpretation of so-called 'minor signs of nervous dysfunction'. No structural correlates are available to validate diagnosis of brain damage. Such signs are considered indicative of an unfavourable condition of the nervous system, primarily on the basis of empirical data showing that such signs relate to generally accepted 'risk-factors', or are more common in children with behaviour problems than in controls.

Furthermore, the difficulties which are commonly associated with neurological impairment in children may have far more to do with the over-all organisation of the child's behaviour than that they manifest themselves in the child's performance at specific, isolated tasks. Eisenberg (1957) suggests three ways in which the neurologically handicapped child may have difficulties with his behaviour which are generally not systematically assessed in standard neurological and psychological examinations.

(1) He may have difficulties in the integration of impressions in relation to time and space, *e.g.* in integrating information about his own body position in relation to the physical environment (for more theoretical discussion see Lashley 1950 and Piaget 1971).

(2) The child may be unable to inhibit unwanted reactions, both on the motor and sensory side. Such inhibition is necessary for the child to be able to give his attention at a consistent level to varying tasks which might be presented to him in school and other everyday settings. In the most extreme cases one may feel him to be a 'victim of his impulses'.

(3) The child's ability to handle a large amount of varying information may be impaired.

These handicaps play a rôle in apparently rather simple visuo-motor acts, such as picking up a block and replacing it. Lashley gives the example of the perception of 'verticality', whereby information about changes in position and motion in the visual field must be continuously integrated with information about the body posture and the tonic activity in the muscles.

A far more complex example is offered by the new experience and the new information that the five-year-old has to cope with when he is introduced to the infant school, when he is expected to form a large number of new social relationships, to accustom himself to a new geographical location which may be very complex and at the same time face new cognitive tasks of a totally different order of complexity to anything he has seen before. In a relaxed situation the child may be able to handle well those cognitive tasks which, in school situations, he found very difficult. For the study of such complex adaptational disorders, objective methods for the observation and measurement of the child's behaviour in all sorts of environments are needed. Especially in the study of such handicaps in younger children, the analysis of so-called 'spontaneous' free-field behaviour may be a strong tool.

One further general difficulty in studying neurology and behaviour is the different approaches of the various disciplines and the different levels of measurement used. In medicine a major problem is the assessment and evaluation of slightly deviant neurological signs, *e.g.* the so-called 'soft' signs. Rutter *et al.* (1970) felt the term 'soft' might qualify at least three different types of phenomena: (1) signs of developmental delay in functions such as speech, language, motor co-ordination, perception, *etc.*; (2) signs either due to generalised neurological disorders or signs of local significance (nystagmus and strabismus may fall into this category, *e.g.*, nystagmus can be due to amblyopia or to labyrinthine disease, and both these would differ very much from that due to cerebellar dysfunction); (3) the third group consists of slight abnormalities which are difficult to detect, such as slight asymmetries of tone, *etc.,* and these signs should not be referred to as 'soft' but simply as signs which are hard to elicit reliably.

Meanwhile, psychology is evolving from a one-sided interest in task performance to a growing interest in the general behavioural organisation of the child. Ethology has provided a strong impetus for such a development. In psychodiagnostics, there is a growing tendency to structure assessment procedures in such a way that they themselves may define the most suitable methods of treatment. In education, methods of teaching are being designed on the basis of principles derived from observations of behaviour both in and outside formal learning situation and from a careful analysis of learning processes. Methods are being developed for the objective evaluation of the effect of management procedures.

However, there are other difficulties. The neurologist and paediatrician are in general looking for abnormalities and cut-off points so that a sign is either 'positive' or 'negative', whereas the psychologist often works with distributions and is much less interested in the definition of pathology. The scope of medical thinking has now increased in that medicine is now not only interested in treatment of illness but also its prevention, as indicated by development of such concepts as 'children at risk'. As

3

clinical research and practice focus more and more on problems related to early detection and the prevention of disorders, behavioural problems are no longer solely regarded as symptoms of underlying diseases, but also as factors in the psycho-social adaptation of the young child.

CHAPTER 2

The Method of Free-Field Observation

This study examines the relationships between neurological findings and free-field* behaviour in pre-school children. The material was collected during one of a series of follow-up studies carried out at the Department of Developmental Neurology in Groningen since 1956.

The relationships between obstetrical and neonatal neurological findings (Prechtl 1968), between neurological findings early and later in the child's development (Dijkstra 1960, Prechtl 1965, Touwen 1972) and the development of neurological functions in the course of the first postnatal weeks (Beintema 1968) have all been explored and standardised methods for neurological assessments have been developed (Prechtl and Beintema 1964, Touwen and Prechtl 1970). The relationship of neurological to psychological and behavioural data, however, is a new and hitherto unexplored subject. The flow diagram (Fig. I) shows how the studies inter-relate.

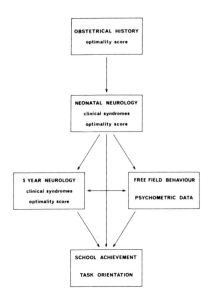

Fig. 1. Flow diagram.

*In a strict sense the term 'free-field behaviour' should be applied only to behaviour in a natural environment. In human as well as in animal research this term is also used to describe the behaviour shown by a freely moving subject in a laboratory setting. In this book the term is used mainly in this last connotation.

Methods of Behavioural and Neurological Assessment

Standardised neurological assessments were related to systematic and detailed observations of the child's behaviour. The study was 'blind' in that the examinations were conducted independently. Examiners had no knowledge of each other's data nor of background data which might have biased them. The neurological examination was based on the techniques developed by Touwen and Prechtl (1970). The children's behaviour was observed in a variety of differently structured environments to allow neurobehavioural associations to show up. It was hoped that the environments used were sufficiently numerous and varied to cover all possible behavioural fluctuations which might occur in the children's natural settings. The environments differed with respect to their familiarity, the presence of other persons, and the amount and types of toys available. These aspects have been shown to be particularly important in modifying the behaviour of normal children of various ages (Arsenian 1943, Rheingold 1969, Hutt 1970, Gershaw and Schwarz 1971, Kalverboer 1971*a*) and they distinguished between children with and without upper CNS lesions in free-field studies by Hutt *et al.* (1965).

Categories have been developed for the description of motor, visual and verbal aspects of behaviour. They allowed for a detailed analysis of aspects such as the child's exploration of the environment, his contact with the mother and his play behaviour (see Chapter 4).

To make these investigations possible, two restrictions were necessary:
(a) Variance in possible determinants of behaviour other than the neurological condition had to be kept to a minimum. To that end the age range was kept as narrow as possible, while data were analysed for boys and girls separately. No special measures were taken to make the group homogeneous with respect to social background. By comparing children from a hospital sample, relatively homogeneous with respect to social background, such differences could be kept to a minimum.
(b) These children were observed in a specially designed playing room which allowed for a strictly standardized observational procedure, instead of in their own natural environments, in which all sorts of uncontrollable environmental changes and unpredictable observer effects may exist.

Before coming to the actual experimental study we shall discuss briefly this observational method.

Observation of Free-Field Behaviour as a Method in the Study of Problem Children

Direct observation

It was not until the second half of the eighteenth century that the child became an object of systematic study. Direct observation of child behaviour was the main source of information in these early studies (Pestalozzi 1774, Tiedeman 1787, Darwin 1877, Preyer 1882). Darwin expressed the opinion that by careful observation of the infant one would see the descent of Man.

Although containing some valuable information, these rather biographical studies were too unsystematic and too biased by theoretical prejudice to be good sources of scientific knowledge. More systematic studies were started by Hall (1891) who developed questionnaire methods to study large groups of children, and they received a strong impulse when Binet began developing methods of measuring intelligence. Objective assessment of the child's cognitive functions was shown to be possible. However, a number of behaviour phenomena, especially those related to emotional and social behaviour, were difficult to quantify. As a consequence, many challenging ideas about child development such as those relating to the effects of sensory deprivation or the effects of an inconsistent social environment in early ontogeny have stayed at the level of unproven opinions.

In the early days the preferred method of study was the strictly controlled experiment which, in its purest form, consisted of holding constant all but one of the independent variables. Such an approach, however, was unsuited to the study of more complex behaviour patterns in relatively unstructured environments, and so naturalistic observations of behaviour became unpopular with students of child development. At best, systematic observation was considered an inevitable preliminary phase before hypotheses could be formulated (Underwood 1957, De Groot 1961). The important scientific part of the study was the experiment, in which specific stimulus-response relationships were observed in circumstances far removed from the natural context.

Bell examined all studies undertaken between 1946 and 1956 and found only two in which parent-child interaction was directly observed (Bell 1964). Since then, the number of observational studies on social interaction has steadily increased to the stage where, as Bell says, 'direct observation might even be seen as an end in itself'.

Ethology, with its emphasis on the observation of free-field behaviour, analysis of behavioural structure and postulation of hypothetical organising systems, gave a strong impetus to this 'back to Nature' movement and observational methods developed in ethology are now used in the study of human behaviour.

It is interesting to note that apart from ethology, another very different factor has led to the renewed interest in the method of direct observation, namely the sharp increase in popularity of behaviour therapy. This statement may seem contradictory because behaviour therapy is largely based on a rather limited S-R model: but behaviourists emphasise the importance of the development of efficient measurement procedures for assessing behaviour-environment interactions in order to obtain base-rate values and to estimate objectively changes due to modification procedures. Authors such as Barendrecht (1969) and Goldfried and Kent (1972) emphasise the importance of analysing the background situation before any modification techniques are applied. They stress the necessity for correct sampling of the observation situations (on the basis of a situational analysis) and the behavioural aspects which are to be studied. Their remarks are particularly pertinent to the study of problem children, where the question arises as to whether generalisations about behaviour in other social and physical environments can be made from observations in clinical settings.

Clinical application of the method of free-field observation

In standard psychological examinations, reliability of results depends largely on the child's ability and willingness to maintain a constant minimum level of attention. Providing this criterion is met, the results may give a valid estimate of the child's cognitive abilities. However, those children described as 'hyperactive', 'distractable' and 'impulsive' may not perform well at assigned tasks due to their task-orientation problems. As these are the very problems that parents and teachers complain about most often, should they not be closely observed and systematically analysed instead of being dismissed as irritating epiphenomena?

In theory, the most valid way of tackling this problem would be to observe the child's behaviour in his natural environment. However, such observations would be very time-consuming and require long adaptation periods; observation conditions would be difficult to standardise and would not lend themselves to experimental study. One approach which may be particularly applicable is that of the observation of the unrestricted child in an environment only slightly more controlled than the 'natural', such as a playroom in the laboratory. With this approach, the selection of proper observational environments and behaviour categories is most important. The study is usually designed in the following way:

(a) The subject receives no specific instructions and his behaviour is limited only by the general structure of the physical and social environment. Introductory remarks to observation situations serve to make them acceptable or predictable.

(b) The behaviour repertoire is described in objectively defined categories. Interpretations of the emotional or other causes of behaviour are avoided in the first instance.

One of the first clinical applications of free-field observation was reported by Ounsted (1955). He describes his first attempts to 'crudely quantify the defects of attention' by 'letting the child run wild in the consulting room and recording and timing the duration of different activities carried out by the unfettered child'.
To quote Ounsted:

'The child was released in a clinic side-room containing a small number of objects—wooden spatulae, an old tin, a teddy, some paper, a couch with blankets, etc. The mother, nurse and doctor stood silent and made no interventions. Each activity made by the child was noted, and the duration of each line of behaviour was timed. Observations continued for five to fifteen minutes at each visit. The conditions of test were occasionally varied by making the test in more complex environments.'

Later, Hutt *et al.* (1963) developed this method further by designing an observation room with a one-way screen and a block pattern on the floor, so that systematic observation and registration of movement patterns could be obtained. Using this technique they studied the free-field behaviour in children with and without upper central nervous system lesions. The children were observed in four situations of increasing complexity; with the room empty, with only blocks present, with blocks and a passive observer, and with blocks and an actively participating observer. Locomotion, attention span and manipulation of fixtures were quantitatively scored from audio-tape recordings and films. There are close similarities between their experimental design and that in the free-field observations in this study.

The interpretation of findings obtained in such laboratory studies depends on (a) the type of environment in which the behaviour is observed, (b) the categories used for the description of behaviour, (c) the way in which registrations are made, and (d) the statistical techniques applied in the different phases of data processing.

8

The selection of observational environments will depend on the kinds of questions one studies and the predictions one wishes to make. Two considerations are of primary importance:

(1) To what extent do the observation situations represent natural environments? (Do they contain the features which are important in the determination of the child's behaviour in daily life?)

(2) Which factors should be standardised and controlled in designing observation studies?

(1) Do observation situations represent natural environments?

It is a well-known problem of developmental assessment in clinical settings that the child's behaviour depends largely on the environment in which the assessment occurs. Children described by parents as 'hyperactive' may fail to show any signs of hyperactivity when seen by the paediatrician in an out-patient clinic; a child examined in a formal testing situation may function far below his optimal level because of the strangeness of the environment. The 'problem of the cage' (Ounsted 1955) exists not only in formal testing situations but also in free-field observations in laboratory settings.

Observational studies of humans are complicated by the fact that each individual functions in a large variety of environments, and general terms like 'home environment' and 'school environment' have different meanings for each individual. All human environments can be considered as more or less 'natural' or 'artificial' depending on one's viewpoint. In designing observational studies one might try to represent systematically the main environmental determinants of children's behaviour instead of simulating all possible daily life environments. These determinants may be identified by considering the sorts of problems the child must cope with daily in his social and physical interaction with the environment. The child must learn to cope with problems of increasing complexity and it is not surprising that factors such as the novelty/familiarity of the environment, the presence/absence of strangers are important determinants of the child's adaptive behaviour. The specific importance of these factors will differ according to the type of problem one is interested in. Situations with strange or unfamiliar people are likely to be the most sensitive in discriminating between children with and without contact disorders, while situations of varying complexity may be most suitable for the study of hyperactive children. In general, children should be observed in a variety of different situations before specific ones are selected for study. This point is illustrated in the case of a five-year-old autistic child and his twin brother. As might be expected, the autistic child looked in the direction of the people present for a shorter time than his twin—a well-known phenomenon in autistic children. However visual fixation of the physical stimuli in the room such as the camera and toys was also shorter. 'Short sampling' was therefore a general characteristic of his way of getting information. Such a finding has important consequences for the child's treatment and could only be found through precise observation in a variety of differently structured social and non-social environments.

At present, very little is known about the consequences of a non-optimal condition of the child's nervous system on his free-field behaviour. Therefore, in the

9

present study, children were observed in a large variety of situations.

Much empirical research will be necessary to clarify the relationships between behaviour in varying environments. As long as such data are lacking one should be most careful in generalising results of laboratory studies to situations in the child's natural habitat.

(2) *Limiting factors in designing observation studies*

A large number of factors may affect the child's behaviour and must therefore be standardised or controlled in observation studies. These factors concern the experimental conditions *per se,* as well as the general context in which the observations occur.

Pilot observations suggested that pre-school children used more different toys and played for longer periods in an empty kindergarten classroom than in a similar room in the research institute, and their behaviour in an unfamiliar room of the research institute was quite different from that in an unfamiliar room of the kindergarten. The child's reactions seemed to be influenced not only by the room but also by the surrounding environment. Seemingly self-evident, this factor is often given too little attention in the interpretation of observational data.

Many factors connected with the experimental conditions may affect a child's behaviour and must therefore be standardised or controlled. A number of these which were identified in pilot studies may be mentioned here.

Minor variations in experimental instruction can influence the child's expectations and so dramatically affect his behaviour. For example, does he expect to stay with or be separated from his mother, to play with attractive toys or be examined by a doctor, to go home after a short or long time?

Various aspects of the laboratory setting may themselves exert a strong influence on behaviour, a fact often over-looked even in well-controlled studies. For example, both adults and children would feel very disturbed when left alone in a room that is sound-dampened. During pilot studies, the different effect on boys and girls of a one-way mirror was noticed, that is to say that with the mother present in an unfamiliar room, the boys showed greater motor and visual reaction to the mirror than the girls (Kalverboer 1971a). Also, a block pattern on the floor seems to encourage movements and games around the room.

Also of importance is the sequence in which the different observation conditions are arranged. A child's adaptation to a new condition will largely depend on whether he has previously been playing with attractive toys or whether he has just been separated from his mother. It was also observed in pilot studies that the child's behaviour was strongly influenced by the type of introduction that he was given to the observation room. When there was the opportunity for the child to get acquainted with the room in his mother's presence he was less easily upset during the rest of the observation than when he had been placed in the unfamiliar room alone—an observation in agreement with the results obtained by Rheingold (1969).

When dealing with children it is important to proceed by gradual stages from a situation where they feel secure, as in the presence of a mother, to the stage where they will feel secure with no mother or other supporting figure present.

10

Physical fatigue and minor illnesses can have a detrimental effect on behaviour and so the general physical condition of the child needs to be considered. A point worth noting is that all the children of this study group visited the toilet before the observation periods began, as small boys in particular become more active when their bladders are full.

It is important to remember that the same environment will affect various individuals quite differently. Some children may find a particular set of toys interesting, while others may show no interest at all. An environment which allows one child to function at his maximum potential may have the reverse effect on another. In general, the objective similarity of the environment may obscure the subjective difference. This factor is of utmost importance for the interpretation of data.

Categories of Behaviour

In observational studies of behaviour, categories should be selected on the basis of explicit criteria. Such categories may refer to (a) the morphology, (b) the function, or (c) the causation of behaviour (Hinde 1966).

(a) Morphology

Morphological categories describe behaviour in terms of spatiotemporal patterning and will include, for example, different kinds of grasp (pincer, palmar, radial) or various kinds of stereotyped movements. In free-field observations, categories such as body posture, locomotion patterns and visual fixations are of this kind. In fact it involves reference to the strength, degree and patterning of muscular contractions (or glandular activity, *etc.*). The method is often limited to a description of the general pattern of limb or body movement, as a complete description would be unnecessarily refined and cumbersome. Thus the detailed muscular contractions involved in running are not described—'running' is usually sufficient. The description of muscular contractions of behaviour will therefore vary in detail depending on one's aims.

There will inevitably be some overlap in this method, as the same action such as walking might be exhibited quite differently in different people, or it might be difficult to distinguish between one category and another. The morphological categories do however provide a relatively objective description of the behavioural repertoire.

(b) Function

Terms such as 'exploration' or 'contact' are functional descriptions of behaviour. Such 'descriptions by consequence' are normally used when the behaviour involves orientation to the environment and when motor patterns, though leading to a constant result, are diverse. Examples are 'approaching the mother', 'exploring the room' and 'seeking contact'. According to Hinde, one of the advantages of this method is that a brief description can cover a multitude of motor patterns. On the other hand, there is also the danger that such descriptions are susceptible to over-interpretation, especially in such a complex animal as the human being.

Morphologically similar actions can have quite different functions depending on

11

the context in which they occur. For example, when a child touches the mirror in the early stages of the observation it is perhaps exploring its environment, but later when the child has become familiar with its surroundings, this action may represent an attempt to vary sensory input. A block pattern on the floor enables one to monitor the child's movements, but whether these movement patterns are those of room exploration or play activity can only be determined by looking at the child's simultaneous eye and hand movements.

One must obviously be cautious in defining behaviour in terms of function, as little is yet known about the meaning of behavioural patterns in different situations.

(c) Causation

Causation refers to the supposed physiological or psychological basis (often called the 'underlying mechanisms') of behaviour. These categories may indicate 'emotions' and 'motives', 'arousal levels' (physiological) and 'organic disorders'.

Descriptions of function and causation will be influenced by the subjectivity of the observer and can often lead to wrong conclusions concerning the physiological or oganic basis of behaviour when no other independent evidence is available. In psychology, psychiatry and early ethological studies there was a feeling that certain morphological patterns had definite functions. It seemed reasonable, therefore, to take a shortcut and describe what was observed in functional terms, with the result that in some analytical writings this functional description became rather fanciful.

Many clinical studies make no distinction between morphology, function and causation and consequently the results of such studies are often inconsistent and sometimes meaningless.

Effect of different measuring techniques and descriptions

Activity scores may differ widely depending on the measures applied and the situations in which behaviour is observed. Wrist-watches (actometers), measures of manipulatory activity and measures of changes of position in space all measure motor activity in different ways. Correlations between the results of several of these different techniques have been found to be low and inconsistent (Cromwell *et al.* 1963). Bell proved that even when similar instruments are used simultaneously on the same person, the scores on each are quite different (Bell 1968). Small wrist-watches were attached to different parts of the body, such as foot and jacket, and in a sample of 37 girls the product-moment correlation was as low as .28. Bell concludes that 'components and manifestations of activity in different measurement situations should be studied, rather than activity as a unique invariant function'.

Another example of large discrepancies between results obtained with different devices is found in a study by Johnson (1972). Johnson simultaneously used an ultrasonic motion-detecting device (described by Peacock and Williams 1962) and photo-electric cells to record walking and sitting. In Johnson's words 'The simultaneous recordings had no predictable relationship to each other'.

Another illustration of the need for explicit criteria in behaviour studies is to be found in the literature on hyperactivity in children. While Rutter found one hyperkinetic child in a study of 2000 (Rutter *et al.* 1970) and Bax found no cases of hyperkinesis in a study of over 1200 five-year-olds (Bax 1972), Stewart on the other hand reports hyperkinesis in four per cent of a group of school children between the ages of five and eleven years (Stewart *et al.* 1966). However, using teachers' reports for a normal population of school children. Huessy reports hyperkinesis in 10 per cent, Wender in 15 per cent and Rutter in 13 per cent (Huessy 1967, Rutter *op. cit.* Wender 1971). From these results it is obvious that quite different criteria are being used. Rutter and Bax refer to a rare pathological condition, the teachers to a relatively common reaction exhibited by children in school and other social situations, for which Bax has coined the term 'over-active'.

The choice between general or more detailed behaviour categories will depend on the problems to be studied. In a complex behaviour problem such as hyperactivity, involving attention, emotion and cognition, a detailed description of the patterning of the behaviour is essential.

In preliminary studies of pre-school children it was observed that girls followed a different strategy in obtaining information about their environment than boys. The girls' visual exploration tended to change in time from scanning to fixation of specific fixtures, whereas in boys the order was reversed. This fact was only discovered because visual scanning and visual fixation were scored as two categories, rather than one general category, i.e. visual exploration.

The use of audio-video recordings considerably increases the scope of the free-field method of observation, as it allows the investigator to re-examine the behaviour categories used in pilot studies and allows for a reliable application of detailed categories in the study of complex behaviour.

In a sophisticated discussion of classification problems Hinde (1971) points out:

'The study of behaviour places the investigator immediately in an inescapable predicament: it demands the use of classificatory categories, but these inevitably falsify reality. To study behaviour we have to name items of behaviour, the external factors which influence it and the processes which supposedly determine it. Naming involves classifying items together into categories, with the implication of discontinuities between the categories: we must therefore be constantly aware of the extent to which our categories really do represent discontinuities, and how far they are a matter of convenience. Furthermore, our categories must be defined in terms of specific criteria, and the nature of these will make them relevant to some problems and not to others.'

From this it follows that for each 'definition in objective terms' a number of more or less arbitrary decisions have to be made, even when distinctions are made on the basis of the morphology of the behaviour. This is inherent to the application of discrete categories for the description of continuously varying behavioural phenomena (Hinde 1971). For instance, the category 'to run' is applied to a number of locomotion patterns, which, though slightly different, have some characteristics which distinguish them from other patterns of locomotion. Categorisation inevitably leads to a certain imprecision in the description of behaviour.

Selection of crucial behaviours
In free-field observations should one select specific elements of behaviour or

13

should one attempt a comprehensive description of the whole behaviour repertoire? The answer, of course, will depend on the aim of the study and the knowledge of the structure of the behaviour. When discrimination between an experimental and a control group is the only aim (for example, between children under a certain drug regime and untreated children) it may suffice to know whether changes in a specific element are theoretically or empirically related to success in treatment. However, little new insight into the relationship between treatment and outcome will be gained by measuring only those changes in one isolated element of the behaviour repertoire. All that can be elucidated is whether a certain treatment affects behaviour, not how it works. As long as the behaviour repertoire of normal children remains unknown, we must continue to record as much as possible of the behaviour repertoire in as many different situations as possible.

Observation in Free-Field and Formal Situations

Systematic information on psychological functioning in children has been obtained in the main through psychometric studies. While detailed knowledge has accumulated concerning cognitive, spatio-constructive, perceptual, speech and language skills, little is known about attention span, activity levels, exploratory behaviour or the child's adaptive behaviour in situations where he is not restricted by specific instructions. The study of these aspects of behaviour is as important as the study of cognitive skills, as the processes involved in formal learning procedures are similar to those involved in the child's adaptation to daily-life situations. Learning disorders are often symptoms of more serious problems evident in all aspects of the child's social and emotional behaviour. (Parents of children with learning disorders often remark that they noticed signs of behavioural disorder long before the child started school.) The individual uses strategies derived from previous experience in his social and physical environment to solve new problems and modifies these strategies on the basis of new experiences; Piaget calls these processes 'assimilation' and 'accommodation' respectively. Montessori recognised the fact that the child learns by exploration and instructed teachers to structure the formal learning situation from what the teacher knew of the child's spontaneous behaviour (Standing 1957).

Appropriately used, the method of free-field observation allows for a refined analysis of complex behaviour, although the limitations of this method should not be overlooked. As stated by Hinde (1966) it is too naive to suppose that the complete behaviour repertoire can be measured objectively. Besides the almost inevitable element of subjectivity, limitations arise from the study procedures and information may be lost due to any or all of the following factors: selection of observation situations; registration of behaviour; choice of behaviour categories; choice of statistical methods and description of results.

However, making allowances for these limitations, free-field observations can provide much valuable information about the behaviour of young children.

CHAPTER 3

Sample, Measures and Neurology

Composition of the Sample

The primary criteria for the selection of subjects were: (a) full term delivery (38 to 42 weeks); (b) birth weight above 2500 grams; (c) complete obstetrical and neonatal neurological records and (d) no severe neurological disorders in the neonatal period. The records of children born in hospital in 1962 and 1963 were examined and 180 cases which fulfilled the above criteria were selected for possible study. Thirty children dropped out of the initial group for the following reasons: 15 were excluded because their families moved out of Groningen; five parents refused to co-operate; two children were ill; two children were too upset to make data collection possible and six parents failed to appear with their children on the assessment day. This left us with a final sample of 150 children, 75 boys and 75 girls. Two children were later excluded at pre-school age due to neurological handicaps. One developed spastic hemiplegia following meningitis and the second child developed oligophrenia after encephalitis. Two more children were brought in to replace them. Therefore, at the time of examination, none of the children suffered from any known physical or mental disorder. However, about 25 per cent had previously suffered illnesses such as febrile convulsions and head injury which carried a risk of producing damage to the nervous system (Touwen 1971). Seventeen per cent had been hospitalised for more than a week.

Obstetrical and Neonatal Neurological Characteristics

As hospital delivery in the Netherlands generally only occurs on medical or social grounds (about 60 per cent), it follows that the present group of children carried a higher risk for obstetrical and neurological complications than the Dutch population in general. In 1968 Prechtl introduced an obstetrical optimality score based on 42 obstetrical factors known to be associated with the later condition of the baby. A baby with a history of none or only one of these factors was regarded as low risk, with two to six factors as middle risk and more than six factors as high risk. Clearly, this optimality concept differs from other concepts of risk. It is fully discussed by Prechtl (1968). Table 1 shows the obstetrical risk groups for boys and girls. In the analyses carried out by Prechtl, relationships between obstetrical optimality scores (based on a number of optimal obstetrical conditions) and neonatal neurological optimality scores were found in a group of over 1,300 cases (Prechtl 1968).

Neonatal neurological examinations were carried out according to the method described by Prechtl and Beintema (1964) which is particularly designed for the neurological assessment of full-term newborn infants, and a neurological optimality score assigned to each child. The optimality score was used as an indication of the integrity of the nervous system in order to avoid the difficulties involved in a normal/abnormal discrimination (Prechtl 1972). Table 2 shows the neonatal neuro-

15

logical optimality scores for boys and girls.

Three syndromes which can be recognised in newborn infants are the hyperexcitability syndrome, the apathy syndrome and the hemisyndrome. These have been defined as follows (Prechtl and Beintema 1964).

Hyperexcitability Syndrome — High intensity of tendon reflexes, low frequency/ high amplitude tremor, Moro with low threshold. Hyperkinesis may also be present, with an increased resistance to passive movement.

Apathy Syndrome — Low intensity and high threshold for responses, hypokinesis and decreased resistance to passive movement. The baby is difficult to arouse and the nervous function is depressed.

Hemisyndrome — When three or more asymmetries are found, hemisyndrome is considered to be present.

Each child is scored in each of these three syndromes using similar criteria to those reported by Beintema (1968).

Eleven children (9 boys, 2 girls) presented with hyperexcitability syndrome, 22 (13 boys, 9 girls) with apathy syndrome and 3 (2 boys, 1 girl) with hemisyndrome. Some relationships between these neonatal syndromes and free-field behaviour at five have been reported earlier (Kalverboer *et al.* 1973).

TABLE 1

Obstetrical risk groups

	Low risk	*Middle risk*	*High risk*
Boys	27	43	5
Girls	14	53	8
Total	41	96	13

Risk groups on the basis of number of non-optimal obstetrical conditions—low risk 0 or 1, middle risk 2 to 6, and high risk 7 or more. No significant difference between boys' and girls' distributions ($X^2 = 5.86$, df: 2, $0.05 < p < 0.10$).

TABLE 2

Neonatal neurological optimality groups

	High	*Intermediate*	*Low*
Boys	33	23	19
Girls	39	16	20
Total	72	39	39

Groups are composed on the basis of the number of optimal conditions—high 37 or more, intermediate 33 to 36, and low 32 or less out of 42 optimal conditions. No significant difference between boys' and girls' distributions ($X^2 = 1.78$, df; 2, $0.30 < p < 0.50$).

16

Timing of the Examinations

The pre-school age was chosen for the follow-up examination for two reasons. (1) Decisions concerning the further school training of the child must be taken at this age. Identification at this stage of children at risk of developing behaviour or learning problems may lead to prevention of more serious disorders later.

(2) At pre-school age children are in a relatively stable social situation. Approximately 95 per cent of the study group had attended a kindergarten for six months or longer. The teachers provided useful information about the child's social behaviour and kindergarten activities. Furthermore, because the child was already used to an environment other than the home, a good adaptation to the laboratory setting was expected. The children go on to school from the kindergarten when they are six.

The Families

Of the 150 children in our group, 146 were living with their own parents. Four children lived alone with their mothers because the fathers had died (two cases) or the parents were divorced (two cases).

Home Circumstances

Eighty-six children lived in the city or suburbs of Groningen (a provincial town of about 165,000 inhabitants), 22 in country towns, 36 in small villages or hamlets and 6 in isolated spots in the country. Eighty-one children had not changed residence for five years, 14 had moved three years or more previously, 37 between one and three years ago and 18 less than a year previously. All these changes of residence were within the same area, generally from the central parts of Groningen to new suburbs.

Birth Rank

At the time of the follow-up examinations 21 children were singletons, 63 were the oldest, and 51 the youngest in the family. Fifteen children were in between.

Kindergarten Attendance

Only nine children were not attending kindergarten at the time of the follow-up examinations. Children in Holland attend kindergarten at four years of age. The normal practice is for the child to start at 8.30 am and stay until 11.30 am and to return in the afternoon from 2 pm to 4 pm. These rather long hours perhaps account for the ease with which the children responded to the long test situations. Only three children were regularly kept home from the afternoon kindergarten because of fatigue.

Age Range

The ages ranged from four years eleven months to five years five months. The exact distribution is shown in Table 3. We naturally tried to keep the age range as narrow as possible in order to prevent the effects of age variation on the results, but some scatter in the ages was inevitable.

There are many other environmental factors that may affect a child's behavioural development. We collected a large amount of social data about the family—for example, whether the family seems to be an 'open' family with much contact with neighbours or whether it was a 'closed' family with very restricted social contacts outside the home. Further social data will be presented separately elsewhere.

The General Procedure of the Follow-up Examination

Approximately three weeks before the date of assessment the parents were sent a written request to participate in the study with the information that a social worker of the department would be in contact with them. Approximately one week later the social worker visited the family and asked them to participate in the study. If the parents accepted, a definite appointment was made, and socio-economic data on the family was recorded by the social worker. One week later, the parents were sent a reminder.

It was explained to the parents that the study would provide information on child development and would help to provide better guidance for parents and children generally. The parents were told that the results would be discussed with them. If treatment and further guidance proved necessary, the parents and children were referred to an out-patient department in the hospital. The parents were asked not to upset their children by letting them know about the hospital visit too early, and were asked to reassure the children of the harmlessness of the procedures. The mother accompanied the child on the day of the examination. (All measures were taken to prevent the child from being scared—no white coats or instruments were in view). We also requested the parents' permission to contact the kindergarten for information on the child's behaviour. The questionnaire to be submitted was first shown to the parents to prevent any suspicion they might have. All parents co-operated.

The Social Background of the Child

The mother reported on the socio-economic status of the family (pre-coded interview) and on her perception of the same (card-sorting), and the social worker gave her personal impression of the family situation (pre-coded interview). (Table 4) This group is below the socio-economic average of the Dutch population, probably because of the specific criteria for reference to the University Hospital for delivery.

The Child's Behaviour in the Home

A written questionnaire on the child's social behaviour in the home was completed by the mother. This questionnaire had been designed specifically for the description of behaviours possibly related to minor nervous dysfunction (Schaefer *et al.* 1965).

The Child's Behaviour in the Kindergarten

A questionnaire similar to that given to the mother was also completed by the kindergarten teacher, with the difference that the teacher also had to complete a questionnaire for a control child matched for sex, socio-economic class and age.

The Medical History of the Child

An interview on somatic aspects of the child's development including the presence of interval complications was conducted by the neurologist using a pre-coded form.

18

TABLE 3

Age range in the follow-up sample

Age in years and months	Boys	Girls	Total
4;11	4	1	5
5;0	11	14	25
5;1	18	25	43
5;2	17	11	28
5;3	10	9	19
5;4	13	13	26
5;5	2	2	4
N	75	75	150

TABLE 4

Socio-economic class (as indicated by the father's occupation)

Socio-economic class	N	%
I (upper-middle)	3	2.0
II (middle-middle)	13	8.5
III (lower-middle)	80	53.7
IV (upper-lower)	44	29.3
V (lower-lower)	9	6.9
no data available	1	0.6

The socio-economic conditions in this group are slightly below those of the Dutch population in general, probably due to the specific criteria for referral to the University Hospital for delivery. (Classification from: J. J. M. van Tulder: Sociale stijging en daling in Nederland, III, 1962, Stenfert-Kroeze, Leiden.)

The Psychological History of the Child

The child was interviewed by a psychologist using a pre-coded form. The questions focussed on social behaviour, language, play behaviour, *etc.*

The Intellectual Development of the Child

The child was given psychological tests involving perceptual, spatio-constructive, cognitive and language skills. The Stanford-Binet IQ test, the Bender-Gestalt test, the Draw-a-Person test, the van Alstyne test, the Frostig test for visuo-motor development and the block design test from the Snijders-Oomen non-verbal IQ scale were given to all children. During all the tests, systematic observations of the children's behaviour were carried out.

A number of observations were also carried out to assess the child's behaviour under time stress and under tasks of varying complexity. Hand preference during visuo-motor tasks was recorded. Results of these examinations and experiments will be published elsewhere; in this report only those relevant to the analysis of the neuro-behavioural relationships will be mentioned.

19

TABLE 5

Intelligence Quotients at pre-school age

	Boys (N = 75)		Girls (N = 75)		Total group (N = 150)	
	M	SD	M	SD	M	SD
Stanford-Binet IQ	104,7	13,7	103,3	13,2	104,0	13,4
Draw a Man IQ	89,8	14,3	94,5	10,6	92,1	12,8

Table 5 gives the intelligence quotients at pre-school age. No significant differences were found between Stanford-Binet and Draw-a-Man IQs in boys and girls. In boys, however, Draw-a-Man IQs are significantly lower than Stanford Binet IQs (p < .05).

Time Schedule on the Day of the Assessment

The complete assessment of each child, always in the same sequence, lasted from nine o'clock in the morning until approximately three in the afternoon. Precautions were taken to prevent the examiners having knowledge of each other's assessment results or obstetrical and neonatal neurological data.

While the child was being tested by a psychology assistant the mother was interviewed first by the social worker and then by the psychologist. After a pause of thirty minutes, the child was given a neurological examination, after which the free-field observations and experiments were carried out. During these observations the medical history of the child was obtained by the neurologist. The day ended with a discussion with the parents on the results of the assessments.

Assessment of the Nervous System

Except for a few minor modifications the neurological examination followed the protocol of Touwen and Prechtl's manual (1970).

The assessment and evaluation of minor signs of nervous dysfunction in children present a number of problems, mainly because it is difficult to distinguish between normal variations in nervous function and minor neurological dysfunctions. A thorough knowledge of changes in neurological functions during ontogeny is therefore indispensable.

In recent years much progress has been made in refining techniques of measuring and interpreting neurological data in children. Although knowledge has accumulated about the normal development of neurological functions, convincing data as to the pathological significance of many so-called 'minor neurological signs' is still scarce. As a result, it is difficult to distinguish between the neurologically normal and abnormal. To avoid making rigid distinctions, therefore, the concept of optimality was used (Prechtl 1968, Touwen 1971). A number of nervous functions were semiquantitatively assessed according to the method described by Touwen and Prechtl (1970). Items and ranges are given in *Appendix I*. By adding the number of items in which the child's performance was within the optimal range, an over-all optimality score and optimality scores for special groups of items were obtained. Not

20

all functions which have been included in the neurological examination contribute to optimality scores because it has not been possible to define an optimal range for all items. It should be emphasised that a non-optimal score should not be regarded as a medical diagnosis of abnormality. Each child was given an over-all optimality score which was taken as a general measure of the integrity of the nervous system. The score represented the number of items out of the pre-determined list of 52 on which the child's score was within the defined optimal range.

For further analysis the neurologist distinguished between a high score (48 to 52) an intermediate score (44 to 47) and a low score (43 or less). The lowest score recorded was in fact 36. Cut-off points between groups were set in order to obtain an adequate number of cases in each group, and were made by the neurologist independently of the results of behavioural observations. Figure 2 shows the number of boys and girls in each score group. Using these groups a preliminary analysis was made to obtain a first impression of neurobehavioural relationships. (See Chapter 6).

Neurological Sub-groups

The over-all optimality score is useful as a global method of trying to look for neurological dysfunction but the clinician will want to look for some sub-groups.

The results of the neurological optimality assessment were examined to see whether non-optimal items clustered. Items were grouped on the basis of clinical criteria and a cluster-and-factor analysis was made (Touwen and Kalverboer 1973). Six sub-groups were defined which may or may not be specific to this particular age group.

Sensorimotor items

The sensorimotor items were: resistance to passive movement; tendon reflexes of the arms and legs; abnormal skin reflex; exteroceptive reflexes on the big toe, *e.g.* Babinsky; threshold tendon reflexes of the arms; active power; threshold tendon

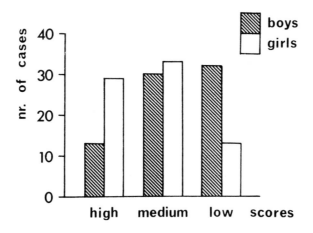

Fig. 2. Neurological optimality at pre-school age.

reflexes of the legs; position of the arms in forward extension and plantar response (Table 6). Of the 101 children who scored one or more non-optimal items, 65 showed signs of hypotonia (symmetrical in 30 cases, asymmetrical in 35 cases). Hypertonia was less common and was observed in only 10 cases. It must be remembered, however, that these children had no clinically recognisable neurological conditions and that the hypo- and hypertonia were detectable solely in terms of non-optimal scores.

Posture

Items of posture were: walking; standing; posture of the feet standing; posture of the legs standing and posture of the feet sitting. The main postural deviations were asymmetries (Table 7).

Co-ordination

The items in this category were: kicking against hand; following objects, sitting; response to push, standing; rebound; finger-tip—nose test and the Romberg test. These items fall into two closely-related groups—those which measure the balance of the trunk (*e.g.* response to push) and those measuring the co-ordination of the extremities (*e.g.* kicking against hand). It was found that approximately 30 per cent of the disorders involved the trunk and 70 per cent the extremities (Table 8).

Choreiform movements

The items of this category were: choreiform movements of arm and trunk muscles; eye, tongue and face musculature and finger muscles. Not surprisingly, the three items measuring choreiform movements were found to cluster (Table 9).

There are, of course, many items in the neurological examination which do not appear in the four groups mentioned, but which should not be omitted from a full neurological examination.

Maturation

Any consideration of neurological functioning in children must take account of maturation and so in this study we studied both *functional maturation* and *maturation of response*. The *functional* aspects studied were: heel-toe gait; rising to sit from supine; walking on the heels; walking on tip-toe; hopping; standing on one leg and diadochokinesia. The results are given in Table 10. The responses studied were: Mayer's response (thumb adduction and opposition on flexion of fourth finger); Leri's response (contraction of biceps following passive flexion of the wrist); the balance response and the plantar grasp. Both Leri's and Mayer's responses appear about the age of four years and should therefore have been present in this sample of children (Table 11). The scores obtained on the two maturational categories were not used in calculating the over-all neurological optimality score.

Table 12 shows the correlations between all six sub-groups. Although the correlations are low, it would appear that sensorimotor deficits do correlate with deficits of posture, co-ordination and maturation. Also, poor co-ordination correlates with poor maturational function and poor maturational responses. Choreiform movements do not correlate with any of the other categories.

22

TABLE 6
Sensorimotor signs

	Number of non-optimal items									
---	0	1	2	3	4	5	6	7	8	9
No. of boys (n = 75)	18	13	10	11	9	5	5	2	1	1
No. of girls (n = 75)	31	17	12	3	5	5	-	2	-	-

Differences between boys' and girls' distributions significant below the 0.03 level with X^2 test and below 0.002 with the Mann Whitney U. Test ($X^2 = 14.33$; d.f. = 6); scores of 6 to 9 non-optimal items were combined for the X^2 test because of low frequencies.

TABLE 7
Posture

	Number of non-optimal items					
---	0	1	2	3	4	5
No. of boys (n = 75)	45	20	6	5	-	2
No. of girls (n = 75)	48	14	7	4	2	-

No significant difference between boys' and girls' distributions ($X^2 = 1.61$; d.f. = 3; $0.50 < p < 0.70$ M.W.U. test p: n.s.); scores of 3 to 5 non-optimal items were combined for the X^2 test because of low frequencies.

TABLE 8
Co-ordination

	Number of non-optimal items					
---	0	1	2	3	4	5
No. of boys (n = 75)	35	26	9	2	2	1
No. of girls (n = 75)	41˙	19	12	3	-	-

No significant difference between boys' and girls' distributions ($X^2 = 2.49$; d.f. = 3; $0.30 < p < 0.50$ M.W.U. p: n.s.); scores of 3 to 5 non-optimal items were combined for the X^2 test because of too low frequencies.

TABLE 9
Choreiform Movements

	Number of non-optimal items			
---	0	1	2	3
No. of boys (n = 75)	12	14	25	24
No. of girls (n = 75)	27	9	25	14

Difference between boys' and girls' distributions significant below 0.05 level with X^2 test ($X^2 = 9.49$; d.f. = 3; $p < 0.05$) and below 0.02 with the M.W.U. test.

TABLE 10
Maturation of functions

| | Number of non-optimal items | | | | | | | |
	0	1	2	3	4	5	6	7
No. of boys (n = 75)	3	4	3	10	13	16	22	4
No. of girls (n = 75)	9	12	10	13	11	11	7	1

Difference between boys' and girls' distributions significant below 0.01 level with X^2 test (scores of 6 and 7 non-optimal items were combined for the X^2 computation; $X^2 = 21.66$; d.f. = 7), below 0.001 with the M.W.U. test.

TABLE 11
Maturation of responses

| | Number of non-optimal items | | | | |
	0	1	2	3	4
No. of boys (n = 75)	17	28	10	13	7
No. of girls (n = 75)	23	31	11	8	2

No significant difference between boys' and girls' distributions with the X^2 test ($X^2 = 5.07$; d.f. = 4; $0.20 < p < 0.30$). A difference below 0.06 was found with the M.W.U. test.

TABLE 12
Correlations between neurological categories (n = 150)

	Sensori-motor	Posture	Co-ordina-tion	Choreiform movements	Matur. of functions	Matur. of responses
Sensorimotor	—	0.25*	0.33*	0.17	0.32*	0.39*
Posture	—	—	0.02	0.10	0.17	0.19
Co-ordination	—	—	—	0.04	0.33*	0.29*
Choreiform movements	—	—	—	—	0.03	0.04
Maturation of functions	—	—	—	—	—	0.32*
Maturation of responses	—	—	—	—	—	—

*Significant below 0.01 level (product-moment correlation two-tailed).

CHAPTER 4

The Free-Field Studies

The free-field studies were conducted at the Department of Developmental Neurology, University Hospital, Groningen. The children were individually observed in a well-lit, air-conditioned room which had been specially designed to resemble that used by Hutt *et al.* (1965). The room was 4.8 metres long and 3.2 metres wide with a block pattern on the floor. The blocks measured 80 cm square as this is the size which has proved most suitable (Hutt and Hutt, *personal communication*). Smaller squares confuse the patterns of locomotion, while larger squares give too little information. The walls of the room were painted a dull green to prevent reflection (Figs. 3, 4 and 5).

A camera and video equipment were placed in an adjacent room and a wall with a one-way mirror fitted into the dividing wall. The observation room was darkened during the video recordings to ensure good quality recording and also to prevent the child from seeing through the screen. A second camera with a wide-angle lens was fixed in a corner of the observation room opposite the one-way mirror, which meant that the child was always within reach of at least one of the two cameras (Fig. 6). The operator selected which camera should be used in much the same way as a television producer would. A Sony video recorder was used to record sound and the entire observation of each child recorded on one tape. A microphone was hidden in the room. On one of the two audio channels on the video tape there was a ten-second time signal (necessary for exact time sampling). Details of the audio-video system are given in Figure 7 and *Appendix II.*

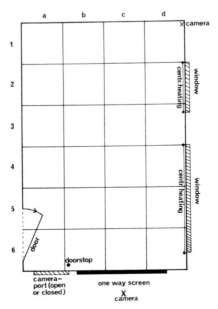

Fig. 3. Plan of observation room.

25

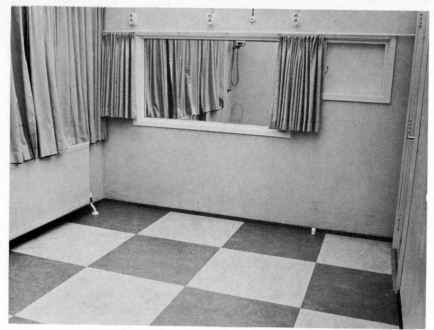

Fig. 4. View of observation room showing one-way screen.

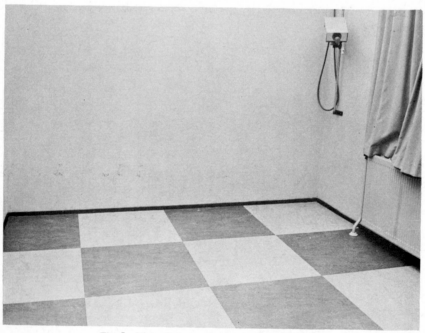

Fig. 5. View of observation room showing camera.

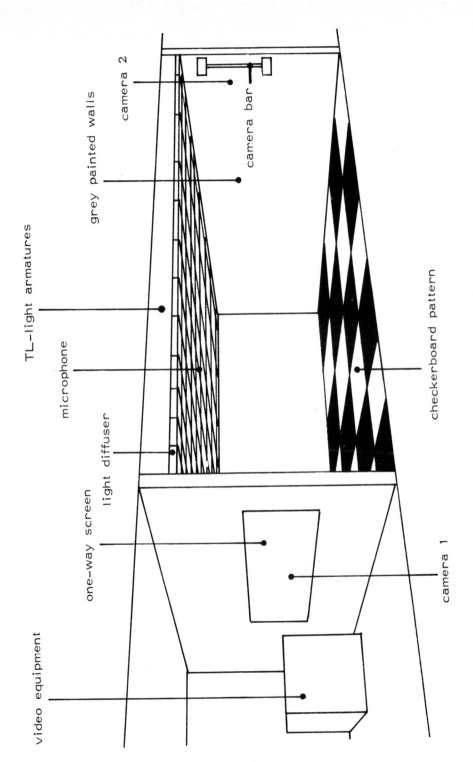

Fig. 6. Schematic representation of observation room.

TL–light armatures

grey painted walls

camera 2

camera bar

microphone

light diffuser

one-way screen

checkerboard pattern

video equipment

camera 1

27

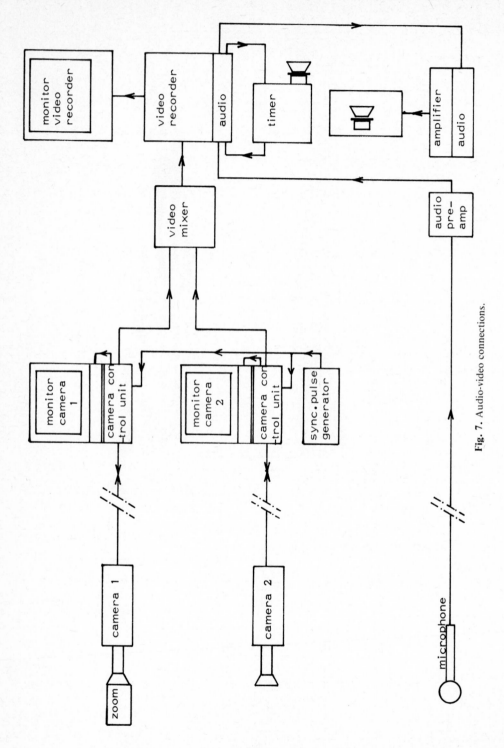

Fig. 7. Audio-video connections.

Pilot Studies

Decisions on factors such as the number of toys to be used, recording techniques, sequence and duration of observations, behaviour categories and presence of other persons were all made on the basis of pilot studies lasting over a year.

One of the main problems that had to be solved was how to keep the child from becoming upset in situations involving separation from the mother or a mild degree of deprivation or external stress (*e.g.* when waiting alone in the empty room, or when alone in the room with an unattractive toy). The pilot studies also helped us to perfect our video-recording techniques and to improve the reliability of the scoring procedure.

Three groups of children were selected.

(1) Thirty children from a kindergarten in the city of Groningen were observed in the laboratory play room and in the kindergarten. From these observations we learnt which of a large set of toys were most frequently selected and the length of time each toy was played with.

(2) Thirty children of different ages and with various neurological handicaps (mainly in- and out-patients from the Child Neurology Department of the University Hospital, Groningen) were observed to determine whether the behaviour categories which had been designed for normal children could also be applied to children with neurological disorders. As a result of this study, behaviour categories were modified and enlarged in order to accommodate a wider variety of behavioural phenomena.

(3) A third group of 30 pre-school-age children was selected from the Department of Developmental Neurology, University Hospital, Groningen. Complete neonatal and obstetrical data were available. These 30 children were similar in age and socio-economic class to the children in the final study.

Design of the Free-Field Study

The mother was told that the child's activities were to be recorded on video tape but she was asked not to tell the child this. All the mothers complied with this request. The recording was started immediately after the mother and child entered the observation room. After the observation period, which lasted 65 to 70 minutes, the mother and child were shown the video equipment and the child watched himself play.

The child was allowed to move around freely during the entire free-field observation. The door was left unlocked but if the child asked to leave the room he was quietly asked to stay. Only when the child was seriously upset (screaming or crying) was the study re-organised or terminated. This occurred with three children when they were left alone in the empty room (Stage 3).

Each stage was preceded by a standardised introduction designed to help the child feel at ease. The introductions were carefully worded so as not to contain any specific instructions which might have influenced behaviour.

The stages in the observation period were as follows.

(1) The examiner says to the child, 'I will look for some toys for you to play with. Please wait here with your mother for a minute.'

The child was left alone with his mother in the empty room for three minutes (Fig. 8). The mother sat on a stool on square a4 and was asked not to interfere in the child's behaviour or to make contact with him in any way. If the child attempted to make contact with the mother, she reacted as neutrally as possible. Handbags and other articles were left outside the observation room in order to make each situation as similar as possible for each child. Although the mother may have felt slightly uneasy at having to sit passively for this three-minute period, her presence was needed in case the child wished to make contact with her.

(2) The examiner enters the room and says to the child; 'Now we are going to do all sorts of things. Your mummy won't be far away and she will be back when we finish playing'.

The mother goes to an adjacent room for an interview with the neurologist. The child is given various formal experimental tasks lasting a total of about 30 minutes. The tasks were performed in the presence of an examiner and in as relaxed an atmosphere as possible, to prepare the child for the next stage. The results of these tests are not described as part of the free-field studies and will be reported elsewhere.

(3) The examiner now removes the test material and says:— 'Please wait a minute. I will get some other things for you. I will be back in a minute'.
The child is now left alone in the empty room for three minutes.

(4) The examiner re-enters with a box of blocks and says:— 'Now you may play with these blocks. Do what you like. In the meantime, I have to do some writing'.

The box of blocks was placed on square b1 and the observer sat on a stool on square d6, making notes and paying no attention to the child (Fig. 9). When the child tried to make contact, the observer reacted as neutrally as possible. This stage lasted 10 minutes.

(5) After removing the blocks, the examiner says to the child:— 'Please wait a minute. I will get some other toys now. I'll bring them in a minute'.
The child is now left alone for a second time in the empty room. This period lasted three minutes.

(6) The examiner now brings a variety of toys into the room saying:— 'These toys are for you to play with. I have to go to another room to do some work, but I will be back in a few minutes'.

The toys were placed in standard positions in the room, after which the examiner left, gently closing the door behind him (Fig. 10). The child is left alone to play for fifteen minutes. The toys were—
a) Cradle with blankets and doll
b) Box containing blocks of different shapes and sizes
c) Garage
d) Paper and drawing pencils
e) Box with construction material
f) Two little cars
g) Truck with trailer (and blocks in the truck)
h) Crane

(7) The examiner re-enters the room, removing all toys except one and says to the child, 'I have to do a little tidying up, but I'll leave one toy here. I'll be back in a few minutes'.

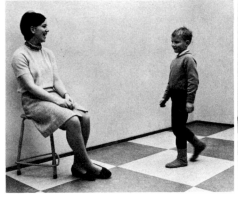

Fig. 8. Mother and child in empty room.

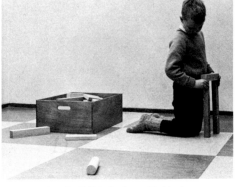

Fig. 9. Child playing with blocks.

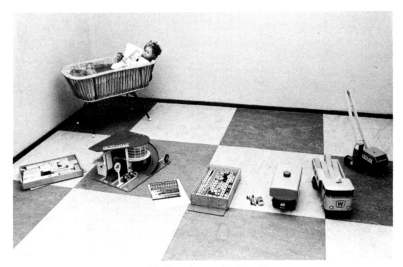

Fig. 10. Toys in standard positions.

The child is left alone for five minutes with the toy which he had previously ignored or had paid least attention to. If several toys had been completely ignored, the selection of one toy was made according to a standard procedure. The cradle was never left because we thought this might prejudice the boys's behaviour. The blocks were most commonly the toy selected.

The first three minutes of the free-field study allowed the examiner to observe the child's reactions to an unfamiliar environment (none of the children had been in the observation room prior to the study). In this situation one expects the child to explore or to be distressed, or both (Arsenian 1943, Berlyne 1960, Rheingold 1969). The pilot studies had shown that in order to avoid severe distress and to maintain the co-operation of the child for later tasks, the presence of the mother would be needed for the first three-minute period in the empty room. This finding is supported by Arsenian (1943), Rheingold (1969) and others who have reported that in unfamiliar

31

surroundings the mother serves as a security base for exploration. We were particularly interested in the relationship between room exploration and mother contact.

The two three-minute periods when the child was left alone in the empty room provided an opportunity for the child to be observed in a situation which had a low level of environmental stimulation and which, because no-one else was present, was mildly stressful. Different groups of children may show systematic differences in behaviour in these circumstances. A child's habituation to such a situation was judged by comparing his behaviour during the first three-minute period of being left alone with his behaviour during the second period.

The child's reactions to the box of blocks (Stage 4) provided information about his selective behaviour when confronted with relatively homogenous material. From the amount of time spent in play, it was possible to estimate the extent of the child's ability to remain oriented to a specific task. Also, the general level of constructiveness of the play was observed, and the way in which body movement related to play activity, for example, whether the child moved more, or less, during play, and whether these movements interfered with his play or formed a part of it. The presence of a passive observer was again needed to prevent children still unaccustomed to the room or disinterested in the blocks, from becoming upset.

After the second three-minute period alone, the child was presented with a set of toys placed in a standard position in the room (Stage 6). The child's selective behaviour in a relatively complex and stimulating environment was observed. Once again particular attention was paid to the level and consistency of play and the relationship between play and gross motor activity. The purpose of the last part of the observation session when all toys except one were removed, was to see how the child reacted to a mildly frustrating situation.

All seven stages of the observation session were designed to relate to aspects of daily life, although this does not imply that the child's behaviour during the study session can be related to his usual behaviour—this will necessitate a separate study. Information about the child's behaviour in home and kindergarten was obtained in questionnaires completed by parent and teacher, but this information was not analysed in relation to the free-field study. Systematic observations of the child at home and at school have not yet been carried out, although our design of the free-field observation was based on pilot observations in nursery schools and at home.

Lastly, as the child's behaviour was influenced by the order of the stages in the study, this order was constant for all children. As a consequence of this, however, such factors as the effect of the mother's presence on the child's initial adaptation (Stage 1) and the relationship between the complexity of a toy and the corresponding level of play cannot be estimated.

Few studies in the past attempted to use an objective, comprehensive description of human behaviour before going on to interpret causation and adaptive function of behaviour patterns (see discussion on page 85 *et seq.*). There were several reasons for this, not the least being the technical difficulties involved. Now, however, with film and video-tape recordings, it is possible to examine behaviour again and again, as was done in this study, and to provide an almost complete and reliable inventory of all observable activity. This is what I attempted in this study. Further, I attempted to use morphological categories, and terms which implied 'description by consequence' were generally avoided. One exception is 'gesture' which seemed a reasonable term to use to describe particular hand and arm movements. Similarly, it seemed reasonable to describe behaviour in terms of environment where different adaptive functions might be confused, for example, looking at persons and looking at objects. It was not always easy to distinguish whether the child was looking at a person or looking at an inanimate object close to him such as the person's clothing. Play level IIE we called 'exploratory' play and clearly there are implications of function in this title but in fact the play was morphologically distinct from the other play categories.

Behaviour was broken down into well-defined categories which were scored according to their duration and frequency. The definitions of the various categories were partly developed from the pilot studies and partly from studies carried out by Hutt *et al.* (1963), Berkson (1969) and McGrew (1972).

Thirty behaviour categories were used. These categories and their definitions are presented on a fold-out sheet so that the reader can refer to them throughout the book (see pp. 126-127).

Locomotion

Locomotion was recorded in three ways.

(1) *Manner of changing position in space with reference to the floor* was recorded by counting the number of blocks covered in 10-second units of time.

(2) *Locomotion patterns* described the simultaneous characteristic structured orientation of the head, trunk and limbs while the child is moving around (Fig. 11). Table 13 gives the different types of locomotion, some of which were defined by McGrew (1972).

(3) Both the number of different locomotion patterns and the number of changes from each pattern to another were recorded for each stage of the study.

Posture

Posture can be defined as a 'specific orientation in space of the head trunk and limbs while the child is not moving around'. Consequently, if the child was given a score for locomotion (*e.g.* running) he would not be given a score for posture. As with locomotion, both the number of different postures and the number of changes in posture for each study were recorded. The postures are listed in Table 14 (Fig. 12). The different postures selected were those most frequently observed in the pilot studies. For similar reasons as with locomotion both the number of different body postures and the number of changes from one to another were recorded.

Manipulation

Manipulation distinguished between manipulation of room fixtures and the child's manipulation of his own body or clothes. Manipulation of fixtures was defined as 'active contact of the hands, feet or mouth with any part of the environment excepting the child's own body or clothes' (Fig. 13). Manipulation of the body is defined simply as 'the movement of mouth or hands with respect to any part of the child's own

33

Fig. 11. From left to right: walk; walking on tip-toe; march; run; hop; jump.

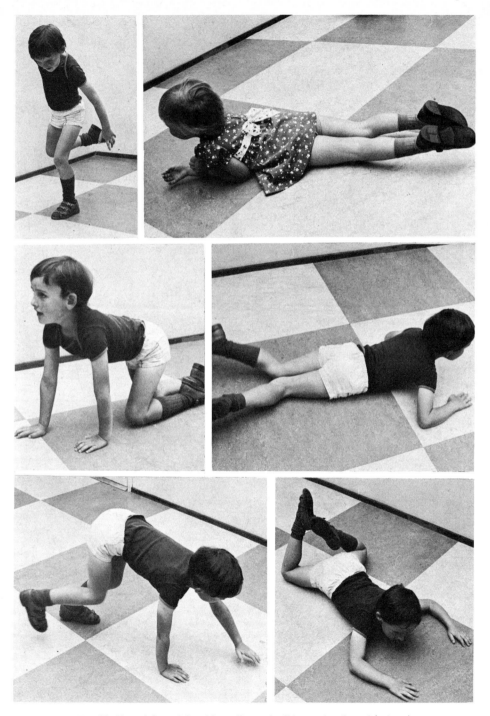

Fig. 11. From left to right: skip; roll; crawl; slide; on hands and feet; swim.

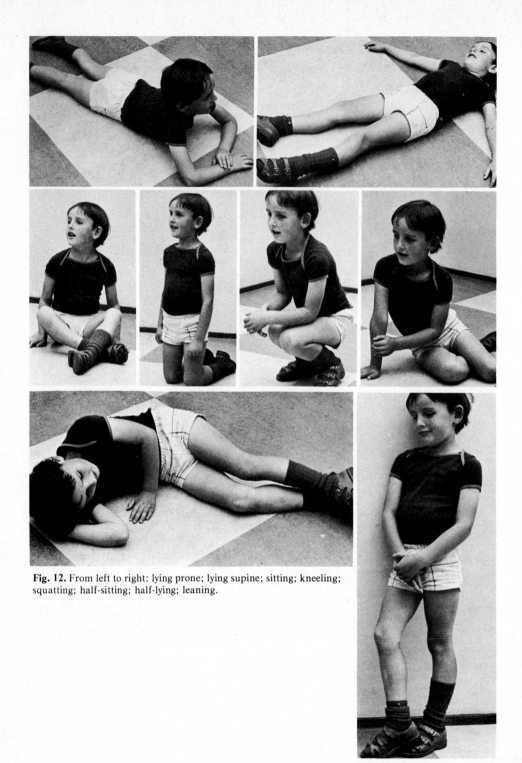

Fig. 12. From left to right: lying prone; lying supine; sitting; kneeling; squatting; half-sitting; half-lying; leaning.

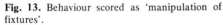
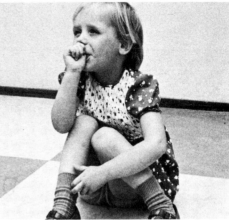

Fig. 13. Behaviour scored as 'manipulation of fixtures'.

Fig. 14. Thumb-sucking and fumbling with socks. This behaviour is scored as 'body-oriented' activity'.

TABLE 13
Precoded list of locomotion patterns

Locomotion pattern	Definition
1) *Walk*	To move the body forward at a moderate pace, alternating legs and placing one foot firmly on the substrate before lifting the other (McGrew).
2) *Walking on tiptoe*	Feet are extended during walking, so that the body is raised and supported only on the toes (McGrew—Kalverboer).
3) *Step*	To move the leg forward once, placing it on to the substrate while shifting part of the body's weight on to it (McGrew).
4) *March*	To walk in a brisk, stereotyped manner with exaggerated movements in an even stride (McGrew).
5) *Run*	To move the body forward at a rapid pace, alternating legs during each stride with both feet off the ground instantaneously during each stride (McGrew).
6) *Hop*	To move suddenly upward into the air by leg or foot extension, landing on one foot in a different location with horizontal motion (McGrew).
7) *Jump*	To move suddenly upward into the air by leg and foot extension, landing on two feet in a different location with horizontal motion (McGrew).
8) *Crawl*	To move forward on hands and knees propelled by the limbs (McGrew).
9) *'Swim'*	To move the body backward, forward or in a circular direction, in constant, frictional contact with the substrate, propelled by the arms (Kalverboer).
10) *Slide*	To move the body in constant, frictional contact with the floor, the hips slightly flexed (McGrew-Kalverboer).
11) *Skip*	To move the body forward by alternating legs, placing one foot on the substrate and hopping slightly on it before shifting the weight to the other foot to repeat the same movement (McGrew).
12) *Roll*	Moving sideward in lying position with continuous rotation of the trunk (McGrew).
13) *Going on hands and feet*	To move forward on hands and feet, propelled by the limbs (McGrew-Kalverboer).
14) *Fall*	The body suddenly and violently moves down from an upright position to a horizontal one, usually on to the ground. The landing is generally on the buttocks or on hands and knees (McGrew).
15) *Other locomotion pattern*	Any locomotion pattern, not included in the list, that can be unequivocally recognized as distinct from other locomotion patterns (Kalverboer).

TABLE 14

Precoded list of body postures

Posture	Definition
1) *Standing*	Upright with both feet supporting the body (McGrew).
2) *Lying*	A reclining posture with the main body axis horizontal to the ground (McGrew). This posture is differentiated in: a) supine: lying on back, torso 0-45° angle to substrate (Berkson) b) prone: lying on belly, torso 0-45° angle to substrate (Berkson).
3) *Sitting*	The body rests primarily on the buttocks. While seated the legs may be extended horizontally, partially flexed with only the feet on the ground, or dangled below. The neck is fully extended with the head upright (McGrew).
4) *Kneeling*	The body rests on the knees (one or both) and feet (both). Other limbs may or may not touch the substrate (McGrew-Kalverboer).
5) *Bending down*	The hips are flexed so that the trunk and head are in a lowered position. Only the feet are in contact with the substrate (McGrew-Kalverboer).
6) *Squatting*	Knees and hips are both flexed, only the feet are in contact with the substrate (McGrew).
7) *All-fours*	The body rests primarily upon the feet and the hands (Kalverboer).
8) *Leaning*	The body axis is approximately vertical. Balance is maintained by supporting the body against the wall, a person, etc. (Kalverboer).
9) *Half lying*	Sideways—reclined posture, with the main body axis approximately horizontal to the floor; usually leaning on elbow (McGrew-Kalverboer).
10) *Half sitting*	The body rests on the buttocks and on one of the elbows (Kalverboer).
11) *Other posture*	Each body posture not included in this list that is unequivocally recognized as distinct from other body postures (Kalverboer).

body' (Fig. 14). The number of manipulations during each stage of the study was recorded.

Gesture

Gesture was defined as 'any communicative movement pattern excluding mouth movement for verbalisation or vocalisation'. It incuded pointing (Fig. 15), waving the arms towards the mother and hand or arm movement accompanying speech. Gestures might appear during play, for example in conversation with the doll, or when talking to an adult in the room. Other types of movement of the upper and lower limbs, head and trunk, which were not part of the patterns of locomotion, manipulation or communication, were scored as 'additional movements'. These included waving the arms and rocking the whole body. Movements directed at the one-way screen (Fig. 16), however, were scored in a separate category as the screen (mirror) exerted a stronger influence on the children's behaviour than any other fixture in the room (Kalverboer 1971a). The children gestured to themselves in the mirror and waved their hands. Banging on the mirror, however, was scored under 'manipulation of fixtures'.

Vision

Vision was recorded in three ways.

(1) *Visual fixation* described the child fixating something but not simultaneously

interacting with it in any other way (Fig. 17). When a child played with an object while fixating it, this was not scored as fixation. It was found in pilot studies that observable visual fixation always lasted at least one second and possible fixation of shorter duration could not be reliably identified. Visual fixation was measured as the number of times and duration in seconds that the child looked at any aspect of the environment for one second or longer.

(2) *Visual scanning* described the child looking around without focusing on any particular object, and was measured in the same way as visual fixation.

(3) *Looking straight ahead* described a child looking in a particular direction without (in the observer's opinion) active visual exploration or inspection. It was measured in the same way as visual fixation.

Because of the high correlations between frequency scores and duration (generally close to 1.0), most duration scores were excluded in the final analyses.

Vocalisation

All vocalisations not regarded as contact behaviour with the mother were scored under two categories. The first (verbalisation) consisted of all meaningful vocalisations and the second (other sounds) consisted of all other vocalisations such as humming, shouting, whistling, *etc.* The first category was initially divided into speech directed towards the passive observer and monologues which occurred during play, but as very few remarks were made to the observer, the two divisions were later abolished. Both types of vocalisation were scored in terms of the number of 10-second epochs during which vocalisations were heard.

Contact Behaviour with the Mother

Contact behaviour was scored during the first three-minute session (Stage 1) when the child was alone with the mother in the empty room. Pilot studies had suggested that various modes of contact with the mother related differently to the child's exploration of the room (Kalverboer 1971a). Active exploration and inspection of the room was frequently associated with talking to the mother (many children gave verbal comments or asked information about features of the room) and children often looked alternately at some fixture and the mother. During the initial phase of this session the children tended to stay near the mother, often touching her and simultaneously scanning the room. Given this information from pilot studies, we distinguished between spatial, tactile, verbal and visual modes of contacting the mother. Initially, contact behaviour was sub-divided into deliberate contact and accidental handling, but this distinction proved too fine and was impossible in practice. Consequently, all tactile contact with the mother was recorded, even when it seemed accidental. An example of this accidental contact is the child putting its hand on the mother's knee while bending down to pick something up. Here the mother's knee may simply be the nearest convenient prop and the child might have used the chair instead. In looking at autistic children under these conditions we have been struck by the way in which the child will make tactile contact but no visual or verbal contact. Often the mother is used as a tool, *e.g.* the mother's hand is brought to the doorknob in order to open the door. In some instances the temporal relationships

39

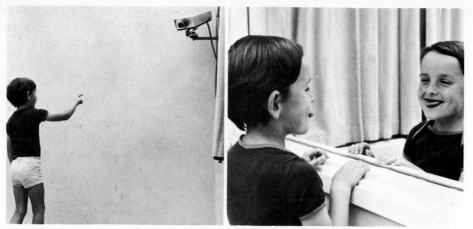

Fig. 15. Pointing at the camera is scored under 'gestures'.   **Fig. 16.** Reaction to one-way screen.

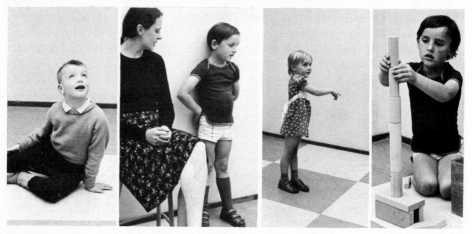

Fig. 17 (*from left to right*): (*i*) visual fixation; (*ii*) looking straight ahead; (*iii*) visual scanning; and (*iv*) in this situation the child is given a score for play behaviour but not for visual fixation.

between the various contact measures may indicate whether a child tries to contact the mother or not, *e.g.* does he look at the mother, or in another direction, while touching her. However, if one is particularly interested in mother-infant contact it would be necessary to make finer discriminations. We tried to standardise the mothers' behaviour by asking them to sit quietly and react neutrally to the child. The amount of contact the mother did make with the child was not in fact measured. However, given these instructions, there were still great differences in the way the mothers behaved towards their children.

Contact behaviour with the mother was divided into four categories.

(1) *Spatial contact* (distance between child and mother) was scored continuously when the mother was present. The mother sat on a stool on block a4 and the other blocks on the floor were graded according to their distance from this block. Block a4

40

scored 3 and the blocks furthest away scored 0. A scoring measure was designed which showed how much time the child spend close to and far from the mother. Few children did both—usually the child either kept close to the mother or felt free to explore the room from the beginning (Fig. 18).

(2) *In visual contact* all 10-second epochs during which the child looked in the mother's direction were scored.

(3) *Tactile contact* described contact of any part of the child's body with the mother, again measured as the number of 10-second epochs in which this occurred.

(4) *Verbal contact* recorded any verbalisation or vocalisation directed towards the mother and was also measured in 10-second epochs.

Tactile contact was initially looked at in two ways:— (1) continuing contact (the child holds his mother's hand for longer than 10 seconds) and (2) frequency of contact. Similar studies were made for visual and verbal contact. It was found, however, that the correlations between the two were so high that in the final analyses only the frequency measures were used. That is to say, a child who tends to have long durations of contact also has a high frequency of repetitive contact. Final scores are not in fact total frequency counts but the number of 10-second epochs in which contact is made. The reason for this is so that comparisons between the different forms of contact could be made more easily.

Level of Play Activity

Most early classifications of play were over-burdened with analytic interpretations (Lowenfeld 1935, Van Wylick 1936, Klein 1960). Play in general has attracted little systematic research. This is mainly due to the difficulties met with in trying to avoid subjective interpretation. There were, therefore, no systematic descriptions available for use in this study. In this study neither the social or emotional elements in play were investigated. I developed a set of categories which attempted to distinguish between patterns of behaviour at various levels of complexity and categories for measuring consistency and duration of play activity. These items are described under the heading 'Other measures of play activity'. All play activity was recorded in seconds.

Play Level I describes a non-specific handling of the material without any observable constructive or symbolic character. This would include activities such as turning the

	a	b	c	d
1	0	0	0	0
2	1	1	1	0
3	2	2	1	0
4	3	2	1	0
5	2	2	1	0
6	1	1	1	0

Fig. 18a. Schema for scoring distance between child and mother.

41

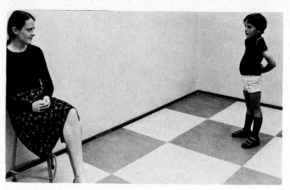

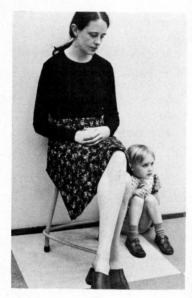

Fig. 18*b* (*left*). The child receives a distance score of 3.

Fig. 18*c* (*above*). The child receives a distance score of 1, and a score for 'visual contact with mother'.

Fig. 18*d* (*below*). The child receives a score in two categories—'gestures' and 'visual contact with mother'.

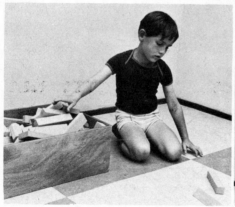

Fig. 19*a* (*left*). Throwing blocks around the room. Level 1 activity.
Fig. 19*b* (*right*). Level 1 activity, unless followed by constructive play.

box of blocks upside down, throwing the blocks around the room (Fig. 19), fumbling in small holes in blocks, rummaging amongst toys without looking for anything, and swinging the doll by one arm without engaging in symbolic play with the doll.

Play Level II was divided into two parts—play behaviour with abstract toys, such as the blocks (Fig. 20), and play behaviour with symbolic toys, such as the doll. Play Level II was defined as play activity determined by the external quality of the material (similarity in form or size) and a number of pre-defined activities directly related to the obvious functions of the toys. These activities, while being more complex than those in Level I, seemed rather aimless and did not suggest that the child was getting involved with play activity as he was in Levels IIE, III or IV. Pre-defined activities in Level II were: making a car go without inspecting it closely and without making any car noises; hoisting the garage platform up and down without putting an object on it; repeatedly opening and closing a car door; casually joining the trailer and truck together; picking up blocks from the box and replacing them; putting parts of construction material together but then later dropping them, and turning a screw of a tanker on and off.

In Level IIE we looked for more involvement in the play material than that of Level II. Level IIE activities seemed to consist of inspecting and exploring the possibilities of the play material. Two examples are, moving a car to and fro while inspecting it visually and looking closely at the blocks to compare their sizes (Fig. 21). The actions were frequently repeated. It was found that Level IIE could easily lead on to Levels III or IV (Fig. 22), while Level II activities usually remained constant. Level IIE activity suggested that a child was becoming interested in some specific material (Fig. 23) and needed to know more about the toys and the ways in which they could be used before employing them in some constructive activity.

Play Level III described constructive activity during which different sorts of toys were not usually combined in an inventive way. Included in this category was phantasy play

Fig. 20 (*left*). During the Blocks condition the observer sits on square d6.

Fig. 21 (*right*). The child compares the sizes of the blocks before using them in constructive play. Level IIE activity.

43

with one toy and also play in which different toys were used in obvious combinations (Figs. 24 and 25). Examples are: attaching a car to a trailer, putting a car on a garage platform and turning the platform down, building a tower from blocks, drawing (as opposed to scribbling which is Level II) and dressing and undressing a doll.

Play Level IV consisted of phantasy play and complicated constructive play where different sorts of toys were combined. Examples are: moving a car into a garage, filling it with oil (Fig. 26), parking it, driving it on to the platform and driving it off to the parking area; making a carefully planned building with the blocks (Figs. 27, 28 and 29); drawing a complex picture (an isolated drawing of a man or circle is Level III). We found that Level IV was often accompanied by verbal explanation, for example, 'the car is going to the garage' or 'the man goes to work'.

We found that children might suddenly change from Level III or IV to Level II. The child would work out a complex sequence of play with the car and, after having put the car on the platform, would suddenly look in another direction, lose interest and then wind the car down in a rather purposeless manner, seeming to forget what he had planned to do next. Simply winding the car up and down was scored as Level II, but if the child started inspecting the hoist mechanism, this was scored as Level IIE.

In order to validate these measures of activity, the IQs of the children were compared with their play scores (Stanford-Binet IQ test). Correlations were generally low. It was found that scores in all high-level play activities correlated positively with IQ. Negative correlation was found between IQ and Levels I, II and IIE (see Table 15).

Other measures of play activity consisted of the child tidying up and putting the toys away. He might, for example, push the truck over to the wall and leave it there, or pack up the blocks and close the lid of the box.

'Changes of play' denoted the number of times a pre-defined activity was replaced by another. A change in play activity did not necessarily involve a change in play level, and a change in play level did not necessarily involve a change in activity. It was often necessary to scan the tapes for a long time before being able to decide on the changes in levels and activities. For example, a child who moved away from the garage and started to build a house with blocks might have changed to a new activity or might possibly have built the house to use it in another game with the car and

TABLE 15

Significant correlations between behavioural variables and IQ

Behaviour variable	r	p (one-tailed)
High level play (Blocks)	+.20	1%
High level play (Vartoys)	+.17	2.5%
High level play (non-motivating toy)	+.16	5%
Body-oriented activity (Blocks)	+.15	5%
Sustained visual attention (one-way screen/Alone 2)	+.14	10-5%
Low level play (Vartoys)	—.27	1%
Gross body activity (Blocks)	—.23	1%
Simple constructive play (Vartoys)	—.18	2.5%
Passive/body oriented activity (non-motivating toy)	—.17	5%
Passive waiting (Alone 2)	—.17	5%
Gross motor activity (Vartoys)	—.16	5%
Low level play (Blocks)	—.15	5%

(Stanford-Binet + Draw-a-Man) N = 150.

garage. A change in play activity usually occurred when the child was with a variety of toys, but could also occur with the blocks or with one toy. The changes were scored as the number of moves from one play activity to another. Frequency of change was supplemented by records of the duration (in seconds) of the longest play activity.

Changing from one toy to another

The number of times that a child changed from one toy to another was recorded. All parts of the doll's cradle including the doll were taken as one toy and this also applied to the blocks, but the two cars were considered as separate toys. Our aim was to contrast and compare changes of toys used with changes in play levels and to measure the extent to which various toys were incorporated in one activity and whether new toys prompted new activity levels. (A sophisticated child usually incorporated many toys in one activity.) The amount of time the child spent unoccupied was also recorded (category 'no play activity'). For further details of play categories see fold-out.

Scoring Procedure

Scoring was done from audio-visual recordings of behaviour. The score sheets were specially designed for the purpose—one for situations with, and another for situations without, play material. Behaviour was scored continuously by two assistants, one of whom gave an oral description while the second filled in the score sheet* (*Appendix III a and b*).

Each observation stage was divided into ten-second sections, the end of each section being marked by an auditory signal on the tape. After each ten-second signal the assistant who was recording the spoken comments of the other moved down one line on the score sheet. Although the observer made every effort to keep up with the recording, some time lapse was inevitable. Slow-motion play-back was used when behaviour changed very rapidly. As only two or three variables could be scored on one play-through, each recording had to be re-played between three and five times before a complete description of the child's behaviour was obtained.

The scoring for all 150 children was done by the same two observers. In order to avoid bias, the author did not take part in the scoring, although he did participate in a number of control scorings to check for inconsistencies in the application of behaviour category definitions.

It took approximately 12 man hours to complete the scoring for each child. The time taken was prolonged because behaviour in certain instances (play activity) was continuously described and was not scored immediately into pre-defined categories. This method allowed for a more flexible analysis than would have been possible using a more rigid system involving fixed behaviour categories.

The results presented in this study are based mainly on total scores for each

---

*'Scoring' refers to the procedure of recording behaviour on the score sheets, and covers both pre-defined categories and continuous verbal description.
'Coding' refers to the process of obtaining data from the score sheets which can then be transferred to punch cards. Most behaviours were pre-coded, but those behaviours recorded verbally (play, locomotion) were coded subsequent to the live study.

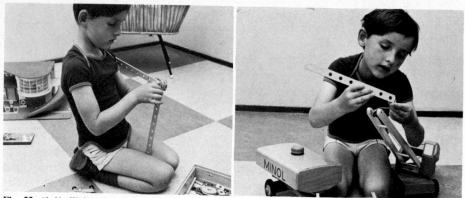

Fig. 22a (*left*). Fixing the parts to each other is scored as Level II or IIE when it occurs as an isolated activity. When integrated in constructive play it is scored as Level IV.

Fig. 22b (*right*). Fixing the bar to the hook is scored as Level III when it occurs as an isolated activity. When integrated in constructive play it is scored as Level IV.

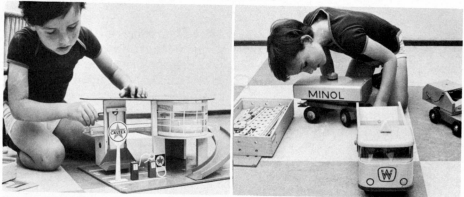

Fig. 23a (*left*). Child tries out the hoist mechanism without the car. Level IIE activity.

Fig. 23b (*right*). Inspecting the car. Level IIE activity.

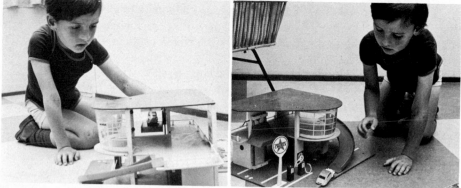

Fig. 24 (*left*). Hoisting the car up and down on the platform is scored as Level III when it is an isolated activity.

Fig. 25 (*right*). Letting the car slide down the ramp is scored as Level III when it occurs in isolation, but when done repeatedly it is scored as Level II or IIE.

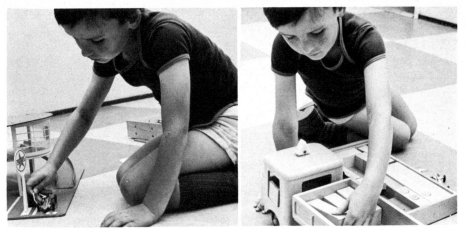

Fig. 26 (*left*). Taking the car to the garage and putting petrol in the tank is scored as Level IV activity.
Fig. 27 (*right*). Loading blocks into lorry and transporting them. Level IV activity.

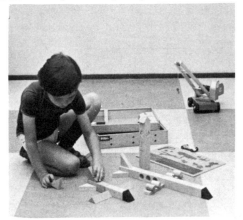

Fig. 28. Building a differentiated aeroplane. Level IV activity.

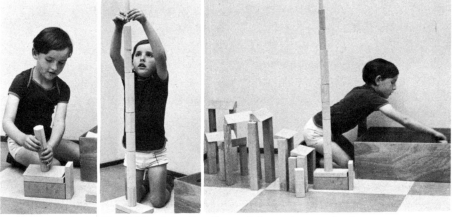

Fig. 29. Three phases of Level IV activity. Note the good visuomotor co-ordination.

47

observation condition and represent either the frequency of occurrence or total duration (in seconds) of a specific behaviour.

A frequency score was obtained either by counting the number of times a particular behaviour occurred, or, by counting the number of 10-second periods during which it was observed. The latter method was used to score behaviours for which a coarse-grained analysis was sufficient (tactile, visual and verbal contact with the mother and vocalisations during play) (See fold-out.). In a pilot study of 20 cases, approximately the same relationships between behaviour variables were found using this simplified method as were found by recording the precise number of times a particular behaviour was observed.

The total amount of time each behaviour was exhibited was estimated by adding up the number of 10-second periods or parts of 10-second periods that the behaviour was observed. This method was chosen because it would have been too time-consuming to measure the exact durations of different behaviours. When two mutually exclusive behaviours such as visual fixation and visual scanning both occurred in the same 10-second period, each behaviour obtained a score of five seconds; when three mutually exclusive behaviours were observed, each obtained a score of three and one-third seconds. The total duration of each behaviour was rounded off to the nearest second.

Spatial contact with the mother was scored according to the square nearest and farthest from the mother which the child entered during each 10-second period. By adding together the 18 nearest and the 18 farthest distance scores, two total scores were obtained. (The mother was present for three minutes, *i.e.* 18 × 10-second periods.) The correlation between these two scores was 0.97, and therefore only one (shortest-distance score) was included in the final analysis.

Behaviour during play was continuously scored on the scoring sheet. From this written description, the number of different play activities, number of toys handled and the level of each play activity, were assessed. (See definitions in fold-out.)

When scoring *locomotion* certain rules were applied in order to assess the child's position on the blocked floor. When the child was positioned on the boundary between two or more squares, the score was determined in the following way:

(a) *when both feet were supporting the body* the score was determined according to the square in which the child's right foot was positioned;

(b) *in a sitting posture* the score was determined according to the square on which the buttocks rested. When the buttocks were on two squares, the position was determined according to the square on which the right side of the body rested;

(c) *in a lying posture* the score was determined according to the position of the trunk;

(d) *for other postures* the score was determined by the square on which the supporting part of the body rested.

For scoring purposes, an arbitrary distinction was drawn between 'visual fixation' and 'visual scanning': when the glance was held in one direction for a second or longer, this was scored as 'visual fixation'; shorter glances were scored as 'visual scanning'.

Reliability Studies

Most previous studies of free-field behaviour in children, particularly in the field of child psychiatry, suffer from inadequate descriptions of various behaviours and lack of concern about the reliability of behavioural data. Although psychological studies have tended to pay greater attention to reliability, the results have a somewhat negative value as behaviour under laboratory conditions may have little relevance to behaviour in a natural, or less formal, setting and often focus only on isolated elements of the behaviour repertoire. With this in mind, considerable attention was paid to the choice of reliable behavioural criteria for this study, and a great amount of time was devoted to the problem in pilot studies. (Full details are given in *Appendix IV*.)

The relationship between reliability and validity must be a close one. Although two observers can reliably identify an isolated behaviour, this is not always the case when the behaviour is part of a complex pattern. Consequently, our reliability studies were made from the audio-video recordings of free-field behaviour and items were scored in the context of the general (complex) behaviour repertoire. Of course, the fact that the observers knew they were participating in a reliability study may have influenced the preciseness of their scoring to some extent.

Procedure

To estimate the reliability of the scoring and coding, fifteen complete video recordings covering all six observation conditions were scored twice. Three different procedures were followed:

(1) Ten complete audio-video recordings were scored independently by the same two observers who participated in the study. The two sets of scores were then coded by one person. This procedure indicated the extent of inter-scorer reliability and thus also illustrated the efficaciousness and objectivity of the pre-defined behaviour categories. (This information may prove useful to those considering the use of these categories in future studies.)

(2) Five complete audio-video recordings were scored by two co-operating observers on two different occasions, six weeks apart. The coding was then done by a third person. For convenience, this procedure was used in the study proper and hence the reliability study and study project were carried out by the same persons. For this reason, the results of the reliability study may be considered indicative of the score reliability of our study.

(3) After all the data for 150 children had been collected, a third study was carried out to assess the reliability of the *coding* procedure. 120 score sheets were coded independently by two assistants, with particular attention paid to Stage 1 (alone with mother in empty room), as all behaviour categories except play were observed in this session.

No formal reliability study was carried out for coding the play behaviour. Instead, three assistants independently scored the play behaviour of 10 children. The three results were carefully compared and decisions were made on the final coding procedure.

49

Appendix IVA shows that inter-scorer reliability was generally high, particularly for motor activity and play behaviour. Further reliability studies will be necessary for those behaviour categories (*e.g.* gestures) in which there were too few scores to make firm conclusions. Undoubtedly, the reliability with which certain behaviour patterns are observed will depend on the context in which they occur. Some variables reliably recorded in the empty room condition have rather low reliability coefficients in play situations, and *vice versa*. Evidently, these differences are due to a change in the observer's focus of attention. Finally, there were very few discrepancies between observers in their application of the various behaviour categories.

Some items were rather difficult to score from the audio-video recordings. Visual contact, in particular, was difficult because 'sender' and 'receiver' were not always on the same screen, and it was often difficult to estimate the direction of gaze (Jaspars *et al.* 1963, Von Cranach 1969, Ellgrin 1969). Nevertheless, correlations were high, probably because the observers were not asked to give precise details of where the child was looking.

The correlation coefficients of the two observers who scored together on two occasions, six weeks apart, were, not surprisingly, slightly higher than inter-scorer coefficients (see *Appendix IVA*).

Reliability of coding

Appendix IVB lists the results obtained when two assistants coded the behaviour of 120 children during Stage 1 (alone with mother in empty room). Inter-scorer reliability was high and so it is unlikely that any discrepancies between scores were due to the coding system. This is particularly important with regard to scores derived from continuous recordings.

No reliability coefficients were obtained for inter-coder agreement in recording play behaviour, but the high inter-scorer and score-rescore agreement may be taken as an indication of the reliability of the coding.

CHAPTER 5

Analysis of Behaviour

In the analysis of the structure of behaviour, a distinction was drawn between *patterns* of behaviour and pre-defined behaviour *categories.* Behaviour *patterns* comprise descriptions derived from basic behaviour *categories,* while the pre-defined categories are those scored by observers from video recordings.

Before the scores could be analysed, a process of data reduction, based on knowledge of the relationships between different aspects of the behaviour repertoire, was necessary. Once these relationships are known, complex behaviour *patterns* can be defined. As a result, the differences in individual behaviour variables between groups can be interpreted with reference to the rest of the behaviour repertoire. To compare isolated aspects of the behaviour of various groups of children without knowledge of how these fit into a general structure may lead to serious misinterpretation.

It is important to be able to return to the original behaviour categories and to be cautious in assuming that, because a child behaves in an apparently identical manner in two different situations, his behaviour in the first situation serves the same function as in the second. For example, fiddling with the room fixtures when left alone with his mother probably represents exploratory behaviour, while this action may serve a rather different function when the child is alone in the empty room—resembling more the fiddling of an adult with a pencil while waiting to be interviewed by a doctor or future employer. The original behaviour categories were analysed very carefully in order to study the relationships between them for different situations. The method is set out in Table 16. This complex diagram represents the most substantial part of our work and should be closely inspected by anyone wishing to carry out a similar investigation (see pp. 52-53).

Column A lists the main steps in proceeding from the definitions of the behaviour categories (A1 in flow diagram) to the description of the behavioural structure (A 13).

Column B lists the control analyses which were carried out to investigate the reliability of procedures, internal consistency of measures, completeness and frequency distributions of data, their experimental dependence, and the appropriateness of the statistical methods.

Column C shows the results of the control analyses, while column D outlines the statistical methods used.

Some of the procedures outlined, for example, comparison of product-moment correlations with rank difference correlations, do not need to be repeated by other workers wishing to duplicate this study.

Because Table 16 is to a large extent self-explanatory, only a few notes have been made (see foot-note below Table 16).

TABLE 16

Flow diagram: steps in the analysis of the behavioural structure

A. MAIN STEPS	B. CONTROL STEPS	C. CONSEQUENCES	D. STATISTICAL METHODS
1. definition of behaviour categories			
2. scores in behaviour categories on protocol sheets (10″ scores)	2/3. determination of a. interscorer reliability b. score-rescore agreement	2/3. improvement of definitions, changes in the observation and registration procedure, etc.	B2/3 and B3. Pearson's PM correlation + T test for differences between means + F-test for differences between variances; control for double zero's
3. sumscores on punch cards (1′- and 3′- scores)	3. c. intercoder reliability		
4. sumscores for separate observation conditions on punch cards (3′-, 5′-, 10′- and 15′-scores)	4. frequency distribution of sumscores for separate behaviours per observation condition	4. decisions with respect to a. missing data b. low frequency variables	
		4/5. removal or lumping of categories	
	5. inspection for 'experimental dependence' of variables		
6. product-moment correlations on selected variables per observation condition	6. rank-difference correlation in one observation condition		A6. Pearson's PM correlation B6. Spearman rho rank-difference correlation
		6/7. PM correlations taken as a basis of further factor and cluster analysis	
7_1. cluster analysis			A7_1. Johnson's hierarchical cluster analysis (diameter and connectedness method)
7_2. factor analysis + rotation (behaviour categories per observation condition)	7_2. factor analysis + rotation in one condition on the basis of rank-difference correlations		A7_2 and B7_2. factor analysis (principal components + varimax rotation)
	7_3. partial correlations	7_3. improvement of the definitions of behaviour	B7_3. partial correlation (first order)

8. definition of behaviour patterns per observation condition	
9. computation of standard scores per behaviour category per observation condition	A9 and A10. Z-scores + summation
10. summation of standard scores	
10. evaluation of correlations, etc.	
10_1. frequency histograms; tests for normality of distributions	$B10_1$. X^2 test on normality of distribution
10_2. estimation of internal consistency of behaviour patterns	$B10_2$. coefficient for internal consistency
11. intercorrelations between behaviour patterns	A11. Pearson's PM correlation
12_1. factor analysis + rotation	$A12_1 = A7_1$
12_2. cluster analysis	$A12_2 = A7_2$
13. behavioural structure: description of relationships between patterns	

C2/3. Since studies on the reliability of the scoring procedure could not be finished before the video recordings in the follow-up study had been started, the results thereof influenced mainly the interpretation of the data, and only occasionally influenced the definitions and scoring. However, the analysis of the intercoder agreement did have a direct effect on the coding procedure in this follow-up study in that a number of behaviours (e.g. 'additional movements' and 'reactions towards the one-way screen') were re-defined on the basis of these results.

A4. The basic data in the study of behaviour consists of the scores in the behaviour categories during all observation conditions.

C4a. Due to technical difficulties during the registration (in particular the sound registration) the data of some subjects were incomplete. The following measures were taken to minimise this effect: (1) application of correlation programs that took into account only the available score (this occurred in the Mother condition, in which auditory information was missing in 13 cases); and (2) substitution by the 'mode' (score of the highest frequency) in those categories in which only a few scores were missing.

C4b. One complicating factor was the low incidence of several behaviours, e.g. crying, gestures. These rare behaviours, although clinically interesting, tended to inflate correlations considerably, and so most of them were excluded from the over-all analysis.

B5. Some variables are experimentally dependent on each other, e.g. locomotion/patterns of locomotion, visual fixation/visual scanning/looking straight ahead, number/types of body postures, number/duration of visual fixations. Scores in such categories cannot vary independently, with the result that correlations between such variables may be strongly inflated. These dependences were avoided by lumping and omitting categories, e.g. changes in body posture and changes in locomotion patterns were combined, and types of body postures, types of movement patterns, looking straight ahead, and a number of duration categories were excluded from cluster-and-factor analysis. However, some variables, although experimentally dependent, were maintained because of their importance in the description of behaviour (e.g. visual fixation, visual scanning and the play-level categories).

A6/B6. Product-moment correlations were applied in the analysis of relationships between categories. As a control in a part of the material, rank order correlations were also computed (Spearman-Rho).

A7₁/A7₂. Methods of factor-and-cluster analysis were used to study the behavioural structure. The differences between these two analyses proved negligible. Behaviour patterns were defined on the basis of these results, on correlations between variables and on the basis of clinical considerations.

B7₃. In some instances, partial correlations were computed in order to rule out the effect of common relationships between variables. For example, during play, a number of behaviours (e.g. reactions towards one-way screen and manipulation of fixtures) only occurred when the child was not involved in play with the toys. By partialling out the category 'absence of play activity', the correlations between such variables dropped considerably. Such partial correlations were taken into account in the definitions of behaviour patterns.

53

Certain aspects of the analysis of the original behaviour categories important for an understanding of the behaviour patterns are discussed in Chapter 4. It should be noted that some correlations are bound to be high simply because scores in certain categories cannot vary independently. Thus locomotion (number of squares covered by the child) and patterns of locomotion are clearly inter-dependent, as are number and types of body postures.

Studies were carried out to examine the closeness of the relationships between these inter-dependent items. Thus the relationship between locomotion and patterns of locomotion was examined by checking to see, whether on most occasions, locomotion consisted of stereotyped locomotor patterns (walking round and round the room) or whether they showed different *patterns* of locomotion on almost every occasion. Many of these analyses are not reported here.

To reduce the number of items in the final analysis, categories were fused or omitted wherever the scores were clearly inter-dependent.

When devising behaviour patterns, attention was paid not only to statistical criteria, but also to the comparability of the behaviour patterns and their relevance to clinical problems.

Relationships Between Categories and the Determination of Patterns

Patterns of behaviour were defined on the basis of descriptive categories used for the coding of data, and identified by the analysis described in Table 16. The following abbreviations will be used to describe the various observation conditions.

Mother — together with mother in novel, empty room
Alone 1 — alone in empty room for first time
Alone 2 — alone in empty room for second time
Blocks — with blocks and a passive observer
Vartoys — alone with a variety of toys
Onetoy — alone with one non-motivating toy

Behaviour patterns in the empty room

Means and standard deviations of behaviour categories and correlations between them are given in *Appendices V* (Mother), *VI* (Alone 1) and *VII* (Alone 2).

The various behaviours of the children in the empty room, with no toys, with and without the mother present, could be put into eight distinct (though not mutually exclusive) patterns.

(1) Exploration of the room.
(2) Reactions to the one-way screen (a variant of (1)).
(3) Passive waiting.
(4) Body movements.* (Body-oriented activity)
(5) Combination of (3) and (4).
(6) Close contact with mother.
(7) Visual contact with mother.
(8) Verbal contact with mother.

*This refers to the child's manipulation of his own body, or other movements not related to the environment.

Our quantitative analysis of the children's behaviour enables us to give a description of the behaviour of the typical child. Although this description might resemble those of previous studies, it differs in that it is based on objectively recorded data.

On first entering the room with their mothers, most children appeared rather timid and passive and were content to stand near their mothers and scan the room with their eyes. After about half a minute they would begin to move away from their mothers for brief periods. As they gradually became more confident and relaxed, they would extend their exploration of the room and fixtures and return to the mother less and less frequently. When the children were left alone in the room for the second time, they had already been in the room for half an hour and had usually become quite accustomed to it. When the tasks set by the examiner (Stage 2) had been completed, most children immediately got up from the table and began to explore the room. Many paid particular attention to the mirror (one-way screen), often standing in front of it making faces and gesticulating. The children tended to spend much longer at the mirror when they were alone in the room than when their mothers were present; when left in the room with their mothers the children would use the mirror to gesture to them. It may be the case that when there was no adult in the room the children spent more time looking in the mirror because the room contained fewer items to stimulate their interest.

There were a number of children who behaved rather passively when left alone in the room and simply waited by the door until the examiner returned. This behaviour may reflect stress. However, very few children became seriously upset when left alone, as they had had time to get accustomed to the room before their mothers left. In some rare instances, children reacted to the Alone 1 and Alone 2 situations with short outbursts of crying, but these rarely lasted more than ten seconds. We saw only two children who broke down and cried so badly that the recording had to be stopped, but neither was in the present sample of children.

(1) Exploration of the room

For all empty room conditions, the following four behaviour categories were taken to indicate exploration: locomotion; changes in body posture and movement patterns; number of visual fixations, and manipulation of fixtures. These four inter-related behaviours correspond exactly to those included in Berlyne's definition of specific exploration, the function of which is to afford access to environmental information that was not previously available (Berlyne 1960).

Correlations between the four behaviours were positive in all three empty room conditions. Correlation coefficients ranged from 0.24 to 0.48* in the Mother condition, but in the Alone 1 and Alone 2 conditions, when the room was more familiar, the internal consistency was lower. This was due partly to the fact that the correlations between 'manipulation of fixtures' and the other behaviours were rather weak (correlation coefficients ranged from 0.11 to 0.35).

*A correlation 0.22 is significant at a 1 per cent level two-tailed (130 to 150 cases are included in this part of the analysis).

There is good evidence from direct observations of behaviour, that the manipulation of fixtures may have a different function when a child is in an unfamiliar environment with his mother than when he is alone in a more familiar environment. In an unfamiliar environment the manipulation of fixtures generally represents inspection, whereas in a more familiar environment it may be a kind of diversion activity. In this context, diversion activities are those which are 'not stimulated by any specific stimuli, but which are resorted to in the absence of novel or interesting stimulation'. It is by the use of this diversion behaviour that a child tries to vary sensory input in an unstimulating environment (Hutt 1970). The finding of an apparent shift from investigation to invention is in agreement with the findings of Corinne Hutt, who observed a similar change in the function of manipulatory behaviour in a group of pre-school children (Hutt *op. cit.*).

(2) Reactions to the one-way Screen

The components of this behaviour pattern are (1) movement towards the one-way screen and (2) duration of visual fixation. In the three empty room conditions, correlations between these two categories ranged from 0.35 to 0.38. The high correlation confirms the impression gained from direct observation, that visual fixations were longer towards the one-way screen than towards other parts of the room. This does not mean, however, that all long visual fixations were directed towards the screen.

Children who reacted frequently to the one-way screen in the Mother condition also tended to spend more time exploring the room (r = 0.54, see *Appendix V*). This was not the case for conditions Alone 1 and Alone 2, where the correlations between the frequency of reactions towards the screen and the amount of time spent exploring the room were 0.12 and —0.02 respectively. This difference suggests that, in the novel room, reactions to the one-way screen were investigatory activities, whereas when the children were left alone, they tended to use the one-way screen to structure their own activity. Direct observations have led to a similar conclusion: in the Mother condition, many children tried to look through the screen and touch its surface, whereas later, in the Alone 1 and Alone 2 conditions, they tended to react to the screen with more inventive behaviour, such as making faces at themselves, pushing out their tongues, and adopting ballet postures.

Despite a high correlation to room exploration in the Mother condition, reactions to the one-way screen have been defined as a separate behaviour pattern because of the specific structuring effect of the screen observed in preliminary studies (Kalverboer 1971a).

(3) Passive waiting
(4) Body movements (Body-oriented activity)
(5) Passive waiting accompanied by body-oriented activity

On first entering the empty room with their mothers, most children tended not to move around. They looked straight ahead and showed (a) body movements and (b) continuous additional movements, which were not directed towards the environment. Visual scanning of the room also formed part of this behaviour pattern which we have defined as 'passive waiting accompanied by body movements'. Correlations between these three categories ranged from 0.20 to 0.48. Body movements, termed 'autistic gestures' by Arsenian (1943) and 'gestures' by Hutt *et al.* (1965) are generally considered to be signs of distress. Visual scanning, as opposed to visual fixation, evidently related to a rather high level of insecurity.

A similar behaviour pattern has been described by Arsenian (1943) who called it 'non-motile withdrawal' (without crying). In Arsenian's study, this behaviour pattern was indicative of a moderately high level of insecurity. In his observations, as well as my own, the pattern of passive waiting accompanied by body movements was frequently seen in children who stayed close to the door or close to their mothers.

When the children were alone in the room, passive waiting and body movements could no longer be considered part of the same behaviour pattern. In the Alone 1 condition, passive waiting and body movements were slightly related ($r = 0.30$) but in the Alone 2 condition they were not related at all ($r = 0.08$) (see *Appendices VI* and *VII*).

Close observation of the way the children behaved when they had had time to familiarise themselves with the room—especially in the Alone 2 condition—strongly suggests that the reason for the statistical relationship between passive waiting and body movements being weak is that the two behaviours have different functions. In the Alone 2 condition, passive waiting seems to be a normal reaction to an unstimulating environment, whereas body movements seem to indicate distress. Passive waiting, therefore, is a reaction to lack of novelty, while body-oriented activity is a reaction to the uncertainty inherent in the situation. In the Mother condition, both behaviours seem to indicate distress. Similar examples of changes in the function of particular behaviours (*e.g.* manipulatory activities) have been reported by Hutt and Hutt (1970).

In some instances, the discrimination between behaviour patterns is strongly determined by the differences between the specific components. For instance, negative correlations between general and segmental body activities determines to a large extent the discrimination between patterns of room exploration and body movements.

(6) *Close contact with mother*

During Stage 1 of the study it was common for the child to stay close to the mother and touch her quite frequently. The two components of this behaviour pattern, spatial and tactile contact, correlate highly with each other ($r = 0.49$). Children who kept close to their mothers tended to behave passively, usually showing body-oriented activity with little inclination to explore the room. Keeping close to the mother seems to be a sign of distress.

(7) *Visual contact with mother*
(8) *Verbal contact with mother*

Visual and verbal contact differed from close contact in the way they related to other aspects of behaviour. The relationship between visual contact and room exploration was weak ($r = 0.22$) while children who waited passively tended to have little visual contact with their mothers ($r = -0.30$). On the other hand, there was no relationship between verbal contact and exploring activities, although a relationship between these two had been found in a preliminary study of 20 pre-school children from a higher socio-economic group (Kalverboer 1971a). These 20 children explored the room while maintaining continuous verbal interaction with their mothers. In the present study, under similar conditions, there was much less verbal contact between child and mother. Other studies have indicated that less verbal coding of experiences occurs in families from the lower socio-economic classes. Tulkin and Kagan (1972) found that middle class infants get more verbal stimulation from their mothers than children from the lower classes.

To investigate the effect of sex differences on the structure of behaviour patterns, factor analyses were carried out separately for boys and girls in the Mother condition. In fact, these analyses showed only slight differences between the structure of the behaviour in boys and girls: factors which explained most of the variance related in boys to room exploration and in girls to body-oriented activities.

As has already been mentioned, some of the eight behaviour patterns defined for Stage 1 (Mother condition) were closely related. *Appendix V* looks at the correlations between these behaviour patterns. It can be seen that there is a strong relationship between the reactions to the one-way screen and room exploration ($r = 0.54$) as both behaviours evidently reflect a tendency to investigate the environment. In the Alone 1 and Alone 2 conditions, when the room was less unfamiliar and reactions to the screen were apparently no longer investigative but diversive, the correlations between room exploration and reactions to the one-way screen were negligible (Alone 1 = 0.12, Alone 2 = —0.02).

Passive waiting accompanied by body movements (seen only in Mother condition) indicated distress, and as commonly observed in children who sought and maintained proximity to their mothers ($r = 0.36$) and who showed little visual contact with them ($r = $ —0.30). Children who spent more time exploring the room tended to look more often in the direction of the mothers ($r = 0.22$). In the Alone 1 and Alone 2 conditions, passive waiting showed a strong negative correlation with the reactions to the one-way screen (Alone 1 = —0.78, Alone 2 = —0.73). Waiting passively seems to be a common boredom reaction to such an unstimulating environment.

Behaviour in Play Conditions

Nine patterns of behaviour were identified under play conditions. These were: low-level play activity; exploratory play activity; high-level play activity; no play activity; gross body activity; room-oriented activity; body-oriented activities (distress); non-specific activities and passive waiting. (Details of frequency of behaviour categories and correlations are given in *Appendices VIII, IX and X.*)

The behaviours that were most commonly observed in each of the toy conditions are described below.

Blocks condition

When presented with the blocks, most children started to play straight away and continued playing for most of the ten-minute period. Some children lost interest in the blocks and some stopped playing and started to tidy them up. Others continued to play in a more random, less constructive manner than previously. Some children stopped playing completely and waited for the observation period to end. Several among this last group complained to the observer, asking how long the period would last, and when they would get something else to play with. Locomotion was generally not integrated with play behaviour in this observation period (see *Appendix VIIIA* and *B*).

Vartoys condition

After the blocks had been removed, the children were left alone in the room with nine different toys. Most children spent the whole fifteen minutes playing and devised lengthy games in which several different toys were incorporated. The girls showed a preference for the doll and cradle, while the boys preferred to play with the car and garage. There was very little gross body activity during this period, although the occasional child walked round the room (see *Appendix IXA* and *B*).

Onetoy condition

Finally, each child was left alone for five minutes with that toy which he had shown least interest in previously. Some children seemed relatively uninterested in the toy (Fig. 30). After playing with it for a while they would wander around the room and fiddle with the fixtures, or simply wait passively. Other children showed quite a high level of play activity (Fig. 31) and spent the entire five minutes playing with the toy. A third group showed only low-level or exploratory play behaviour. Several showed signs of distress, some cried and in two cases we were obliged to intervene before the five-minute period was over. (*Appendix XA* and *B*.)

(1) Low-level play

The widest range of play levels and types of play activity was observed during the Vartoys observation session. The most primitive behaviour pattern of this session was low-level play, when the children threw the toys around and banged them on the floor, or piled the blocks up haphazardly. Frequent switches from one activity to another

Fig. 30 (*left*). Onetoy condition. The child pays no attention to the blocks.
Fig. 31 (*right*). Onetoy condition. The child plays constructively.

were characteristic of this level. Low-level play was seen in all the play situations with slight variations in pattern depending on the number and types of toys available in each situation.

The components of low-level play are (a) non-specific handling of toys (Level 1), (b) simple constructive play (Level II), (c) number of play activities and (d) number of changes in the level of play.

Correlations between scores in these four categories ranged from 0.13 to 0.33 in the Blocks condition, from 0.21 to 0.40 in the Vartoys condition and from 0.23 to 0.46 in the Onetoy condition.

(2) *High-level play*

A pattern of high-level play existed in all play conditions (Levels III and IV (see *Appendix XI*). Examples are: building a tower with blocks; dressing and undressing a doll; moving a car into a garage, filling it with petrol and parking it, *etc.* This level of play is characterised by the inventive and constructive use of toys and also incorporates phantasy play using one or more toys. In the Onetoy and Vartoys conditions, this type of play was related to long periods of play activity ($r = 0.46$ in both conditions).

(3) *Exploring the toys*

Only in the Vartoys condition did most children explore the toys. A child might open and close a car door repeatedly, or turn the screw of a tanker off and on. In the Blocks and Onetoy conditions, such activity was regarded as low-level play. The activity of exploring the toys correlated negatively with constructive play and positively with the non-specific handling of toys.

(4) *No play activity*

The amount of time each child spent unengaged in play was recorded. Several authors (*e.g.* Arsenian 1943) consider a short duration of play to be a sign of distress. In the present study short play durations were observed both in children who showed signs of distress and in those who did not.

(5) *Room-oriented behaviour*

Room-oriented behaviour was seen only in the Onetoy condition. The children showing this behaviour pattern did not play with the available toy; they manipulated the fixtures of the room, gestured at the one-way mirror and generally moved around the room in a variety of different movement patterns and postures.

Correlations between these different behaviours (when the variable 'no play activity' was partialled out) were significant only in the Onetoy condition, which is to say that only in that play condition did these behaviours form a general pattern.

Due to the different functions of behaviours in different situations, the behaviours which were considered a part of room-oriented behaviour in the Onetoy situation were considered a part of exploratory behaviour in the Alone 1 and Alone 2 situations. In the Onetoy situation the child engages in room-oriented activities in an attempt to vary sensory input to avoid boredom (Hutt 1970), indicated by behaviours such as manipulating fixtures without looking at them, simply moving around, *etc.*

(6) *Body-oriented activity*

These movements were seen only in the Blocks condition. They included thumb-sucking and playing with personal clothing, and were sometimes accompanied by rocking movements or crying. They were generally considered signs of distress in the child. The fact that this behaviour occurred only in the Blocks condition was probably because the children found the blocks rather uninteresting. Correlations between the component behaviours were significantly positive when the variable 'no play activity' was partialled out.

(7) *Gross body activity*

Gross body activity (frequent changes in posture and movement patterns) was seen as a specific pattern only in the Blocks and Vartoys conditions. In the Onetoy condition this was part of the pattern of room-oriented behaviour. There was a positive correlation between the component behaviours in both the Blocks and Vartoys condition (Blocks, $r = 0.52$, Vartoys, $r = 0.78$).

In the Onetoy condition the amount of gross body activity was specifically related to the amount of room-oriented behaviour, whereas in the Blocks and Vartoys conditions, the amount of gross body activity was related to the amount of play activity. Children who moved around a lot during the Blocks and Vartoys conditions tended to play inconsistently and at low levels. Thus, there were positive correlations between gross body activity and low level play (Blocks, $r = 0.23$, Vartoys, $r = 0.37$) and negative correlations between gross body activity and high-level play (Blocks, $r = -0.35$. Vartoys. $r = -0.25$). (See *Appendix XI*). Gross body activity is obviously not a part of constructive, high-level play. Further investigation of this relationship may provide interesting insight into the adaptiational problems of so-called 'hyper-active' children.

(8) *Non-specific activities*

Non-specific activities ('additional' movements and vocalisations) were confined to the Vartoys condition, and were seen in those children who were not occupied with the toys. They may be considered diversion activities.

(9) *Passive waiting accompanied by body-oriented activities*

This was seen only in the Onetoy condition and is perhaps self-explanatory: the children spent much of their time looking straight ahead, or about them, sometimes playing with their bodies, thumb-sucking and rocking to and fro.

Results of factor-and-cluster analyses confirm the impression derived from the correlation matrices that connections between categories in the three play conditions were generally low.

Children's Behaviour in Different Environments

Can one predict the behaviour in one environment from observation of that

61

behaviour in another environment?

It was found that correlations between similar behaviour patterns in different observation conditions were generally low. Significant correlations were found between the following behaviour patterns (See Appendix XI):

	correlation
room exploration in all empty room conditions	.23 to .35
reactions to one-way screen in all empty room conditions	.16 to .29
body-oriented activity in all empty room conditions and Blocks condition	.16 to .30
gross body activity in Blocks and Vartoys cons.	.44
no play activity in all play conditions	.14 to .33
low-level play in all play conditions	.10 to .27
(*exploratory play* relates to low-level play in the Vartoys condition)	.19 to .23
high-level play in all play conditions	.14 to .25

No relationships were found between the patterns of *passive waiting* in the various conditions.

Only occasionally were correlations above .35. *Children's behaviour may clearly be quite different depending on the situation in which it occurs.* Moreover, the correlations refer to the behaviour of the group as a whole, and do not permit any conclusions about the predictability of the behaviour in the individual child.

From the few significant correlations between differently defined behaviour patterns, the following are the most interesting.

(1) Room exploration in the Mother condition is associated with gross body activity in the Blocks condition (r = .37) and Vartoys condition (r = .30) and with room-oriented behaviour in the Onetoy condition (r = .24). This result is due partly to the fact that the category of gross body activity is included both in room exploration and room-oriented behaviour.

There were weak relationships between room exploration in the various empty room conditions and between duration of play and amount of exploratory play in the Vartoys condition. Correlations ranged from .17 to .32. This second relationship is interesting in that it suggests that a tendency to explore the environment may be a rather consistent characteristic in some children.

There were some significant correlations between mother contact and various other behaviours. For example, children who kept close to their mothers tended to show little exploratory activity in the Alone 1 and Alone 2 conditions (r = −.19 and −.22 respectively). These children also frequently manipulated their own bodies and clothes and played less in some play conditions (correlations around .23). These results, however, give only weak support to the general idea that children's behaviour in new environments allows for predictions about their behaviour in other situations.

Of all the variables used in this study, 'no play activity' in the Vartoys condition related most strongly to other behaviours. Children showing long play durations in the Vartoys condition

(a) explore the room a great deal and show few body movements in the empty room conditions

(b) show long play durations in the Blocks and Onetoy conditions

(c) show little close contact with the mother.

All correlations range from ± .20 to ± .40.

Summary

In the group as a whole, consistency of behaviour was remarkably low. Significant correlations ranged from ± .20 to ± .35, which indicates that scores have only 4 to 12 per cent variance in common, that is to say, one would have little success in trying to predict behaviour in one situation from knowledge of that behaviour in another situation. At best, sub-groups of children can be identified, characterised by specific combinations of behaviour patterns in the six observation conditions. In the following chapter we will attempt to identify these sub-groups using a method of profile analysis.

CHAPTER 6

Free-Field Behaviour in Relation to Sex and Neurological Condition

Introduction

In this chapter results of the analysis of neurobehavioural relationships will be presented.

For the following reasons, boys' and girls' data were separately analysed:

(a) Behaviour and learning problems that might be related to CNS disorders are much more frequent in boys than in girls.

(b) More minor neurological dysfunctions are reported in boys than in girls (Stemmer 1964, Wolff and Hurwitz 1966).

(c) Several authors (e.g. Bell et al. 1971, Wolff and Hurwitz 1973) stress the necessity to analyse neurobehavioural data separately for boys and girls, because relationships may be different in both sexes. Wolff and Hurwitz state: 'any generalizations applied to all children that are based on an examination of either males or females alone must be viewed with suspicion'.

(d) Preliminary analyses suggested that not only might neurobehavioural relationships be stronger in boys than in girls, but that the kinds of relationships might also be different (Kalverboer 1971b, Kalverboer et al. 1973).

Therefore in this section data will be presented on differences between boys' and girls' free-field behaviour, and how these possible differences relate to the neurological condition will be briefly discussed. Profile analysis was one of the methods used in this study and this technique will be briefly explained.

The Method of Profile Analysis

Profile analysis allows individual children to be sorted into groups which display characteristic behaviour patterns in the various different situations. Thus the results of the profile analysis in this study allowed us to identify three groups of children in general, one forming a non-exploratory group, another a general group, and a third group characterised by a great deal of exploration. The methodology of profile analysis is complex, but some brief notes are given here for the guidance of readers who are not familiar with this method.

Latent profile analysis has been described by Gibson (1959) as the generalisation to quantitative data of latent structure analysis (Lazarsfeld 1950). According to Gibson (1962), latent profile analysis of intercorrelations among variables divides a group of subjects into a number of sub-groups (latent classes) for each of which the profile of standard score means on the various variables is given. These latent profiles are then to be compared and interpreted with respect to the kinds of people they characterize. The latent profile model attributes all observable covariation among the variables to variation between the latent classes, so that within-class variation in each of the sub-groups is, by definition, statistically independent (local independence). This may be illustrated by the following example.

The matrix below contains the comparatives of scores on two dichotonous variables (E is exploratory activity and C is contact with mother scored in a yes/no fashion) as they were found in a group of children.

Table a — Explor.

Contact

	+	−	
+	8	13	21
−	16	7	23
	24	20	44

For this group there is a significant negative correlation between the scores in both variables (r_{EC} = .31). Let us assume that this relationship is due to the fact that the group is composed of two sub-groups with quite different reaction patterns (*e.g.* one group which shows much exploration and little contact, the other the opposite). Table b and c, derived from Table a are an example of such a finding.

Table b — Explor.

Contact

	+	−	
+	5	1	6
−	15	3	18
	20	4	24

Table c — Explor.

Contact

	+	−	
+	3	12	15
−	1	4	5
	4	16	20

When such sub-groups really exist the method of profile analysis is able to identify them. As shown in Table b, there is no longer any correlation between the two variables, exploratory and contact, in each of these sub-groups (local independence).

The original purpose of the method was to discover traits, tendencies or dispositions which might underly variation of phenomena (Lazarsfeld and Henry 1968). Mårdberg (1971) applied the method for the description of data. He states: 'the method is particularly applicable in exploratory studies, in which the aim is to develop previously unknown profile constellations'. This is also the way in which I applied the method. No normality of distributions of scores is required. Mårdberg (1974) gives the most complete description of the method.

Skewness, and curvilinearity of relationships contribute to triple-correlations which are used in the discrimination of profiles. This is an advantage over some other types of profile analysis (Crinella 1973) which use product-moment correlations so that information is lost when distributions of scores deviate from normality. In the programme developed by Mårdberg and applied in my study, no statistical test for 'local independence' is included. Therefore hypotheses about 'underlying dimensions' cannot be tested—its use is restricted to the description of data.

65

To determine how many profiles should be extracted from a set of data one has to define reasonable criteria. I used the following:

(a) Standard deviations of variables in the profiles should be as small as possible. To achieve this, successive analyses were carried out on the same data, deriving a different number of profiles on each occasion. That analysis was selected in which standard deviations of components were the lowest. This criterion guarantees that groups represented by such profiles are relatively homogeneous.

(b) The number of cases per profile should not be lower than four. This limit was chosen because of my interest in the general rather than in the individual nature of the relationships sought.

According to the definitions given in Chapter 4, the term *behaviour pattern* refers to combinations of related categories to which labels are applied such as 'room exploration', 'low-level play', 'body-oriented activity', *etc.* The term 'behavioural' or 'neurobehavioural profiles' refers to groups of children characterized by specific associations between behavioural patterns or between neurological measures and behavioural patterns combined.

Children with Characteristic Behavioural Profiles in the Six Environments

Three groups of children, characterized by different combinations of behavioural patterns in the six observational environments, are represented in Figure 32. In this analysis only those pre-school children were included who had complete behavioural records in all six observation environments (N = 117).

Three profiles could be identified, labelled as 'exploration', 'non-exploration' and 'general'.

The 'exploration' profile (a) includes 24 children (21 per cent of the group). They typically show a high amount of room exploration or other room-oriented activities, such as reactions towards the one-way screen. They usually play at a low level with much gross body activity.

The 12 children (10 per cent of the group) in the 'non-exploration' profile (c) show a quite different behaviour. They react passively with a high amount of body-oriented behaviour when the room is empty or the toys are not attractive, while the total time spent in playing tends to be short. They keep close to their mothers in the novel room.

The 'general' profile (b) contains 81 children (69 per cent of the group), who are characterized by scores around the group-mean in all patterns, except those related to the level of play activity; they play longer and at a level slightly higher than the group as a whole. Evidently the result is directly linked to the rather low levels of play activity in the 'exploration' and 'non-exploration' groups.

The most interesting finding is that inconsistent play at a low level is found both in children with high as well as in those with low amounts of exploratory activity in the empty room. However, the behaviour during playing is quite different in these two groups of children: children in the 'exploration' profile move around in the room a great deal with many changes of body postures and movement patterns, whereas children in the 'non-exploration' profile show a more passive type of behaviour, paying little attention to the toys.

Sex Differences

Behavioural profiles

Table 17 gives the number of boys and girls in each of these three general behavioural profiles (Fig. 32).

TABLE 17

Sex distributions in the behavioural profiles (N = 117)

Profile	Boys	Girls
I Exploration	21	3
II General	35	46
III Non-Exploration	5	7

$X^2 = 15.1$, p $<$ .01

I-II, X^2: 14.6, p $<$ .001; I—III, X^2: 8.4, p $<$ .01; II-III, p:ns.

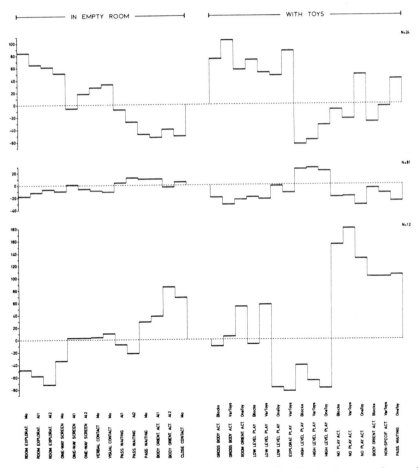

Fig. 32. Behavioural profiles to which all 30 behaviour patterns defined in the six observation conditions contribute.

The sex distribution over the profiles deviates significantly from the distribution to be expected by chance ($X^2 = 15.1$, df: 2, p < 1%). The difference is mainly determined by the large number of boys in the 'exploration low-level play' profile, 21 boys versus 3 girls. No difference in the number of boys and girls is found in the non-exploration profile. As a consequence the number of girls is slightly higher in the general profile (35 boys versus 46 girls). This result is to some extent in agreement with data reported by Hutt (1966, 1970), who observed more 'explorers' among boys in relation to a novel object and more 'non-explorers' among girls.

Behaviour patterns

A more detailed comparison of the behaviour of boys and girls in this group can be made on the basis of behaviour patterns (Fig. 33).

Significant sex differences are found in all observation conditions. They show a consistent pattern, different in empty room and play conditions.

How boys and girls behave in the empty room

Together with the mother in the novel empty room, boys spend more time in exploring the room and talk more frequently to the mother than do girls. As indicated in previous analyses, the patterns of 'exploration' and 'verbal behaviour' are closely related: the child explores the room in continuous verbal contact with the mother,

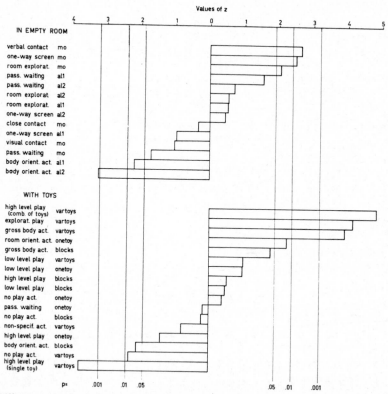

Fig. 33. Differences in behaviour patterns between boys and girls. Bars to the right indicate higher scores for the boys; bars to the left indicate higher scores for the girls.

especially during the first minute (Kalverboer 1971a). Interestingly enough, in the next observation condition (alone for the first time in the empty room), more passive waiting is observed in boys than in girls, a difference due to a much sharper decrease in exploratory activity in boys than in girls.

In all empty room conditions more body-oriented behaviour is observed in girls than in boys. This difference is most pronounced in the condition 'alone in the empty room', due to an excess of body manipulation in girls. Previous analyses strongly indicate that this behaviour is a sign of discomfort (Kalverboer 1971a).

How boys and girls behave in play conditions

Differences in the play conditions concern the amount of gross body activity, as well as the level and the duration of play activity. In all play conditions the boys show more gross body activity than the girls (p = 1% in the variety of toys condition, p = 5% in the condition with blocks, and p = 3% in the condition with non-motivating toy), whereas the level of play activity is generally slightly lower in the boys than in the girls. In the play situation with blocks, more passive behaviour and signs of discomfort are observed in the girls than in the boys. This is a similar difference to that found in the empty room situation. It suggests blocks are more attractive to the boys than the girls.

Behaviour categories

Behavioural differences between the sexes are detailed in Table 18, in which the basic categories directly scored from the video recordings are compared. They show that manipulative exploration in particular is much more frequent in boys than in girls, especially in the novel room and for the first time alone in the familiar room (p < 1%). In the novel room girls show more visual scanning than boys, who spend more time in fixating specific aspects of the environment, often prior to manipulation. Detailed observation reveals that as a group the boys show a slightly different pattern of gathering information about the environment than girls: boys tend to start with looking at specific aspects of the environment, whereas girls tend to scan the room visually before looking closely at specific fixtures. Perhaps girls feel more tense and distressed in this laboratory setting than boys, as suggested by the relationship between visual scanning and signs of discomfort reported in the preceeding chapter. In the play situation the differences between the boys and the girls are more apparent than real. The boys have more Level IV play, but this is because they tend to use several toys together. The girls have more Level III activity because they tend to concentrate on one toy, such as the doll and its cradle. (Doll play may be scored as Level IV or as Level II, see Fig. 34).

Interestingly enough in the empty room conditions no differences between boys and girls are found in the amount of locomotion. Also 'close' contact with mother does not discriminate between boys and girls.

In summary, differences between boys' and girls' free-field behaviour are evident in empty room as well as in play conditions. However, the similarities between the boys' and girls' behaviour are much stronger than the differences. In all conditions boys' and girls' behaviours largely overlap. This is also indicated by results of a profile analysis of behaviour in each of the six observations separately. From the 19 profiles which could be identified, there are only two in which the distributions of boys and girls differ significantly from the sex distribution in the total group of 117 children—one 'low level play, gross body activity' profile in the condition with a variety of toys (31 boys versus 12 girls, $X^2 = 10.34$; df 1, p < .001), and one similar profile in the condition with blocks (17 boys versus 6 girls, $X^2 = 9.72$; df 1, p <.01).

TABLE 18
Behaviour categories: differences between pre-school boys and girls in the six observation conditions.

	Mo	Al 1	Al 2	Blocks	Vartoys	Onetoy
1. Locomotion				+ +	+ + +	+ + +
2. Changes in body posture		+		+ +	+ + +	+ + +
3. Types of body postures	+	+		+ + +	+ +	+ +
4. Changes in locom. pattern				+ + +	+ + +	+ +
5. Types of locom. patterns				+ + +	+ +	
6. Additional mov. (discr.)		+	+	+	— —	
7. Types of addit. movements		+	+		— — —	
8. Gestures	+ +					
9. Mov. tow. one-way screen	+ +			—		
10. Manip. of fixtures	+ + +	+ + +	+ +			+
11. Types of fixt. manip.	+ + +	+ + +	+			
12. Manip. of own body/clothes	— —	— — —	— — —	— — —	—	
13. Visual fixation (nr.)	+					
14. Visual scanning (dur.)	— —					
15. Tactile cont. with mother						
16. Spatial cont. with mother						
17. Visual cont. with mother						
18. Verbal cont. with mother	+ +					
19. Sounds				+	+ + +	
20. Absence of play act. (dur.)					— —	—
21. Longest play act. (dur.)					— — —	
22. Nr. of toys handled					+ + +	
23. Types of toys handled					+ + +	
24. Changes lev. play act.					+ +	
25. Changes type play act.					+ + +	
26. Play act. Level I (unspec. handling of toys)						+ +
27. Play act. Level II (low construct.)					+ + +	
28. Play act. Level II (explor. of toys)					+ + +	— —
29. Play act. Level III (high constr. one toy)					— — —	— —
30. Play act. Level IV (high constr. several toys)					+ + +	
31. Tidying up					— — —	

The 'N' for the boys is 71 to 75 and for the girls 69 to 72. '+' equals more in boys, '—' equals more in girls. One sign (+ or —) gives a 5-10% p value, two signs (+ + or — —) a 1 to 5% p value and three signs (+ + + or — — —) a 1% value (all on Mann-Witney two-tailed).

Fig. 34. Various phases of playing with doll. A sequence of activities such as dressing and undressing the doll and putting it to bed is scored as Level IV; when these activities occur in isolation they are scored as Level III. In the bottom right-hand corner the child is poking her finger into the doll's eye. Such behaviour often occurs as an interruption during Level IV activity and is scored as Level II or IIe.

71

Neurobehavioural Relationships in Boys and Girls

Do differences between boys' and girls' behaviour relate to their neurological status?

Are differences between boys' and girls' free-field behaviour partly due to neurological differences? Some preliminary data on this problem have been reported (Kalverboer *et al.* 1973). Free-field behavioural categories were compared in boys and girls with low optimality scores as well as in boys and girls with high optimality scores, derived from their neurological examinations. Between the boys and girls with high optimality scores differences in amount and variability of gross motor activity were found in only two of the observation situations (Blocks and Vartoys), whereas between non-optimal groups such differences were present in each of the six experimental conditions: boys with low optimality scores invariably showed more changes in body postures and movement patterns than low-scoring girls, irrespective of the presence of play objects. This was mainly an effect of the inconsistency of motor activity in the boys with low optimality scores, something not found in the other groups. In other words, only in boys with low optimality scores were inconsistencies in motor behaviour observed irrespective of the specific structure of the environment, whereas in the other groups, changes in body postures and locomotion patterns were primarily related to the play activity.

In random samples more minor neurological dysfunctions are found in boys than in girls. Therefore, differences in neurological condition may partly account for behavioural differences commonly found between the sexes. However, more detailed analyses will be necessary to answer this question.

Preliminary analysis: optimality groups

The purpose of this analysis was to get an initial impression of the significance of the neurological condition for the child's free-field behaviour. For full details of differences between separate categories see Kalverboer 1971*b*, Kalverboer *et al.* 1973.

In a preliminary analysis groups were compared which differed with respect to their over-all neurological optimality scores: a high score group (48 or more out of 52 optimal conditions), an intermediate score group (44 to 47 optimal conditions), and a low score group (36 to 43 optimal conditions). Cut-off points between groups had been set by the neurologist in order to obtain a sufficient number of cases in each group and independent of results of behavioural observations. Details are given in *Appendix I* and Chapter 3.

Neurobehavioural relationships were stronger in boys than in girls. They partly concerned different aspects of the behaviour and were observed in different kinds of environments.

In the boys, differences between optimality groups were mainly observed in the Alone 2 and Onetoy conditions. In particular the amount of exploration and the level of play activity discriminated between neurological groups. However, behavioural differences between boys with higher and lower neurological scores were not consistently in one direction, but depended on the structure of the environment. As long as the room was relatively unfamiliar, most exploratory activity was shown by boys with an unfavourable neurological condition. However, when the child was acquainted with the environment (for the second time alone), boys with low optimality scores behaved most passively and had evidently lost interest in the environment. Similar differences, although less pronounced, were found between neurological groups in the girls. This is illustrated in Fig. 35 for one of the main aspects of the exploratory activity, *i.e.* visual attention to fixtures in the room. These results suggested that boys and girls with low optimality scores need more variation in environmental stimulation to remain attentive than groups with a more favourable neurological condition.

Another difference between neurological groups in the boys concerned the level and duration of play activity in the three conditions with toys. In the Onetoy and Blocks conditions, boys with low neurological scores played at a lower level than groups with more favourable scores. However, when there was a variety of toys available just the reverse was observed: boys with the lower neurological scores played at a higher constructive level than others. The data indicated that boys with an unfavourable neurological condition may function quite well when the environment provides sufficient stimulation, whereas their level of functioning drops below that of controls in a non-stimulating situation.

More detailed analyses showed that, in particular, measures for the inconsistency of the gross body activity, such as changes in body postures and locomotion patterns, discriminated between the neurological groups in the boys (Kalverboer 1971*b*).

Differences between neurological groups in the girls were weaker and less consistent than in the boys. They mainly concerned the contact behaviour in the novel empty room: girls with optimal neurological status kept closer to the mother and presented more signs of distress than girls with low scores. The last group reacted more frequently towards the one-way screen and explored the room more intensively. Such differences were not found between neurological groups in the boys.

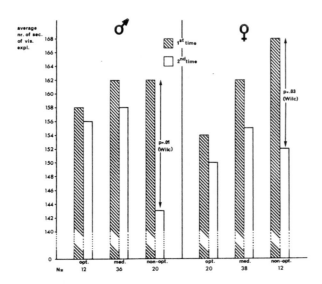

Fig. 35. Average time spent in visual exploration during the first and second time alone in the empty room. The drop in visual exploration reaches significance only in the non-optimal groups (Wilcoxon two-tailed).

73

The data indicated that observation conditions and aspects of the behaviour which discriminated between optimality groups were partly different in boys and girls. In boys, minor neurological dysfunctions seemed to affect the behavioural organization, particularly in environments with a low level of sensory input, whereas in girls the strongest discrimination was found in an unfamiliar situation with an opportunity for social support.

In this preliminary analysis, groups were compared which differed with respect to their over-all neurological optimality scores. However, the optimality groups are heterogeneous with respect to their neurological symptomatology, whereas cut-off points between groups had been arbitrarily set. Nervous functions contribute quite differently to the optimality scores in different children. Inconsistent findings may be partly due to the heterogeneous composition of the neurological groups. Minor disorders in motor co-ordination, choreiform dyskinesia, or difficulties in sensori-motor integration may differ as to how they affect the behavioural organization.

More differentiated analyses are necessary to clarify these neurobehavioural relationships. To that purpose, profile analyses were carried out in which the neuro-logical measures were introduced. The various neurological sub-groups in Chapter 3 were used in this analysis.

Neurobehavioural profiles

Variables included in the analyses

Results of profile analyses in which neurological as well as behavioural variables are included are given for boys and girls in the Figures 36 to 42 for each of the conditions in which the children were observed. The following neurological categories, each composed of a number of items, are included in these analyses.

1. sensorimotor
2. maturation of functions
3. maturation of responses
4. choreiform movements
5. co-ordination
6. posture

These neurological categories are described in Chapter 3, and the correlations between them are given in Table 12.

Items from two of them, 'maturation of functions', and 'maturation of responses', were not included in the neurological optimality scores which were applied in the analysis discussed in the previous section. Each child obtained an 'optimality-score' for each of these neurological categories. The more 'non-optimal' items, the lower the score in that particular category (in the graphs they move below the zero line).

The behaviour patterns defined in each of the six observation conditions are included in the profile analysis together with these neurological categories.

Neurobehavioural relationships were analysed in boys and girls separately. To facilitate comparison of results, data of both sexes are given in the same figures. Detailed data concerning the discrimination between neurological and behavioural measures in the various profiles are given in *Appendix XII* (t values indicate meaningful differences).

(In the text we refer to low neurological scores as non-optimal scores and high scores as optimal scores. However the terms are not quite literal: a high score is a departure from the mean for the group on which the analysis has been made and is in the direction of optimality and not necessarily optimal in an absolute sense.)

Neurobehavioural profiles in the empty room conditions — With mother in the novel empty room

In boys as well as in girls two neurobehavioural sub-groups could be distinguished, as represented in Fig. 36. In essence the profiles are similar in both sexes. However, only, in the girls do both neurological and behavioural measure contribute substantially to the discrimination between groups, whilst in the boys the profiles are only discriminated by the free-field behaviour measures. This result may indicate that the aspect of 'unfamiliarity' may be particularly important for the behavioural discrimination of neurological groups in girls.

Behaviourally, children with non-optimal (low) neurological scores (39 boys, 26 girls) are characterized by a high amount of exploratory activity and many reactions towards the one-way screen, whereas those with higher scores (22 boys, 30 girls) behave more passively and keep close to the mother. In the boys there is also a difference in amount of verbal and visual contact with the mother which is most frequent in those with the lower neurological scores. This verbal and visual contact

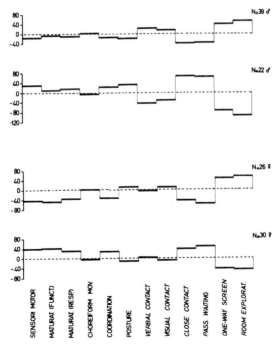

Fig. 36. Neurobehavioural profiles in the Mother condition. Boys' and girls' data were analysed separately. Neurological variables are to the left, behavioural variables are to the right. Optimal scores have a positive value.

behaviour is directly linked to the inspection of the room while the child tries to communicate with the mother about his impressions.

In the girls the maturation indices are strongly associated with the behavioural measures. Choreiform dyskinesia has no implications for the behaviour in this situation, neither for boys or girls.

For the first time alone in the empty room (Alone 1)

Neurobehavioural profiles are given in Fig. 37. Two profiles were distinguished in each sex group.

In this condition in which the environment is already familiar to the child, different neurobehavioural relationships are found in boys and girls. In boys the group with the low neurological scores (28) shows the highest amount of room exploration, paying much attention to the one-way screen, while those with high scores (33) typically show more passive and body-oriented behaviours. In girls, however, the situation is somewhat reversed, in that girls with the lower neurological scores (20) are the most passive group, paying less attention to the one-way screen and showing more body-oriented behaviour than those with higher scores (36). Most of these girls were in the group of the 'explorers' in the previous condition with mother.

In the boys, all neurological categories (except maturation of functions) contribute to the distinction between groups. In the girls, just as in the previous condition, choreiform movements and posture do not contribute to the discrimination.

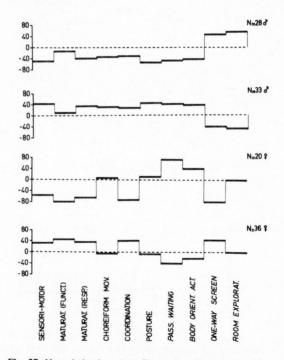

Fig. 37. Neurobehavioural profiles in the Alone 1 condition.

For the second time alone in the empty room (Alone 2)

After the session with blocks (described in the next section) the child is for the second time alone in the empty room for three minutes. In that condition neuro-behavioural relationships are again approximately similar in boys and girls (see Fig. 38).

In both sexes children with unfavourable neurological scores (15 boys, 19 girls) typically show a pattern of passive waiting. Children with high neurological scores (46 boys, 37 girls) pay much attention to the one-way screen, whereas especially in the boys other features of the environment such as the camera and central heating are explored. In this condition, all neurological variables except choreiform movements contribute to the neurological discrimination in the girls. In the boys the categories 'posture', 'sensorimotor', and 'maturation of responses' are the most important.

These differences in patterns of exploration and passive waiting suggest that in an environment with a low level of stimulation, children with an unfavourable neurological condition lose interest more quickly than those with a more favourable neurological condition.

Neurobehavioural profiles in the play conditions

In all play conditions meaningful associations were found between neurological findings and behaviour. More profiles could be distinguished than in the empty room conditions, so that results give a more differentiated impression of the neuro-behavioural relationships.

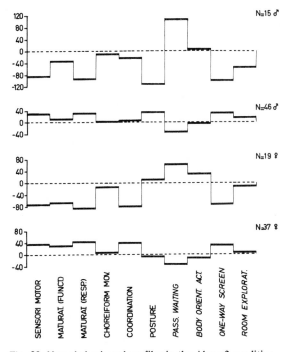

Fig. 38. Neurobehavioural profiles in the Alone 2 condition.

With blocks and a passive observer (Blocks)

Neurobehavioural profiles are given in Fig. 39.

The profiles show that there is a connection between the child's neurological status and the level of playing with the blocks. In both sexes, groups with unfavourable neurological scores (36 boys, 20 girls) typically show many activities of a low level, such as throwing blocks away or simply piling them up. In the boys, low level play is typically connected with much moving around and short durations of playing, which is not the case with girls.

In boys with favourable neurological scores (25) much constructive play is observed: they play quietly and for relatively long periods. In the girls two different behaviour patterns were found in association with favourable neurological scores. One group of boys (28) typically shows play activity at a high level, being involved in longer play periods than the group of girls as a whole. The other group of girls (8) shows little involvement in playing and much body-oriented and gross body activity.

Neurologically, in the boys choreiform dyskinesia contributes more than any of the other variables to the discrimination between groups. This is in strong contrast to empty room condition where choreiformity was of no significance.

This result suggests that there is a specific relationship between choreiform dyskinesia and the quality of one child's constructive play. This is confirmed by correlations in the boys of $-.42$ and $+.26$ between measures of choreiform dyskinesia on the one hand and high and low level play on the other, as found in previous analyses. Such correlations (which do not exist in the girls) are among the highest in the whole material.

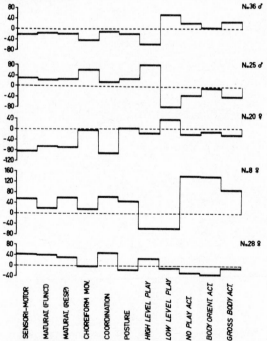

Fig. 39. Neurobehavioural profiles in the Blocks condition.

With a variety of toys (*Vartoys*)

In this condition two profiles were distinguished in each group. In contrast to results in other play conditions, boys with low neurological scores (25) show more constructive play at a high level and play longer than those with high scores (N = 36). In the group with high scores more non-specific behaviour (see Fig. 40 and Appendix IX) and gross body activity occurred than in the group with low scores. The results suggest that in boys with an unfavourable neurological condition the level of functioning is positively affected by the variety and attractiveness of these toys. They further indicate that neurological dysfunctions may have quite a different effect on the behavioural organization in situations with and without a high amount of stimulating input.

Such a difference in relationships between play activity level in different environments and neurological status is not found in the girls. Just as in the condition with blocks, the level of the play activity is the lowest in girls with unfavourable neurological scores (26). They show more exploratory play and play at a lower level than girls with high scores. In the favourable neurological group (30) more high level play is seen, whereas they are slightly less involved in playing than the girls with low neurological scores.

With one non-motivating toy (*Onetoy*)

This mildly distressing condition gives the most interesting results. Ten neuro-behavioural profiles representing rather homogeneous groups could be identified, four in the boys and six in the girls. They are represented in Fig. 41 for the boys and in Fig. 42 for the girls.

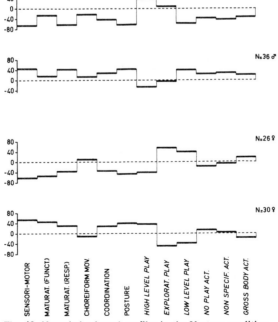

Fig. 40. Neurobehavioural profiles in the Vartoys condition.

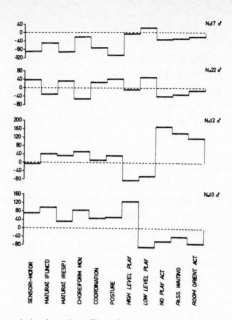

Fig. 41. Neurobehavioural profiles of the boys in the Onetoy condition.

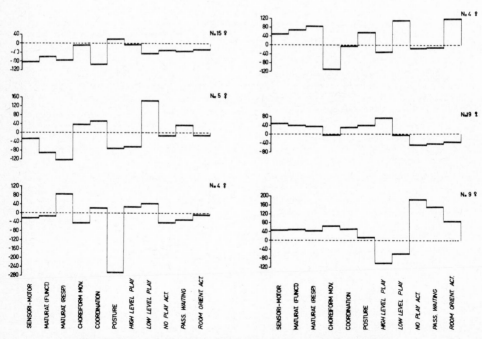

Fig. 42. Neurobehavioural profiles of the girls in the Onetoy condition.

80

The four groups of boys are clearly distinguished from each other, neurologically as well as behaviourally.

The same pattern of profiles emerges for the boys in this condition as was found for the girls in the condition with blocks. Different types of behaviour are seen in the two groups of boys with favourable neurological scores. One group (10) with high scores in all neurological categories shows high level play and concentrates mainly on the play material, while the other group (12) plays for shorter times and, when not playing either waits passively or shows room-oriented activities. In the boys with lower neurological scores (17 and 22) low level play of short duration is typically seen. Both groups show more play activity and less passive behaviour and room-oriented activities than the average of the group. The group of 17 boys has low scores in neurological variables, whereas in the other group of 22 boys choreiform dyskinesia and signs of dysmaturity (functions) are prominent.

In the girls two groups were identified with high scores in five of the six neurological variables (9 and 19). Their behaviour is similar to that of the two groups of boys with high neurological scores and is also similar to that shown by girls with high neurological scores in the Blocks condition. In one of these groups (9) little involvement in playing and a high amount of room-oriented and body-oriented behaviour is observed, while the girls represented by the other profile (19) tend to play at a high level and longer than the group average.

Two groups of girls could be distinguished with specific neurological characteristics. Four girls with choreiform movements but scores above or at the average on the other neurological variables are behaviourally characterized by a high amount of low level play and many room-oriented activities. Inspection of the raw protocols of these children indicates that they spend more time in manipulating fixtures in the room and show more changes in body postures and movement patterns than the group average.

Four other girls have low scores in posture and a few signs of choreiform dyskinesia. Behaviourally these children play slightly longer than the average of the group, while they are not distinguished from the other children in the other behaviours. The girls represented by the two other profiles have low scores in most of the neurological variables. One group of five girls with non-optimal signs in the categories 'maturation of functions', 'maturation of responses' and 'posture' plays at a low level and tends to behave passively. The other group of fifteen girls has low neurological scores, except for choreiformity and posture, and shows less low level play and plays longer than the other group.

Conclusions

Profile analyses provide a differentiated and meaningful picture of the relationships between neurological and behavioural variables in this group of pre-school children.* They confirm the general notion that there is no fixed relation-

---

*It is difficult to compare results of profile analyses in different observation conditions because numbers in the groups change at each occasion. Some further indications about neurological differences between groups follow from data in App. XII in which means and t-values are given.

ship between neurological condition and behaviour, but that such relationships depend on the nature of the situation to which the organism is exposed.

In girls, neurobehavioural relationships are stronger and more like those in boys using this profile analysis than found by optimality group comparisons. This may be partly due to the inclusion of the maturation categories which are particularly significant in the girls.

Compared with children who have favourable neurological scores, children with unfavourable scores typically show a greater amount of exploratory activity in an unfamiliar environment, followed by a greater decrease in such activities on later exposure to a similar environment. A decrease in amount of exploration occurs earlier in the observation procedure in the girls (in the Alone 1 condition) than in the boys (in the Alone 2 condition).

Close contact with the mother is commoner in girls with favourable neurological scores than in girls with unfavourable neurological scores.

In the play conditions the main results are as follows.

(1) Two sorts of behaviour are typically observed in children with favourable neurological scores:—

(a) behaviour characterized by little involvement in playing and much body and room-oriented activity, and

(b) behaviour characterized by a high level and long duration of play activity.

(2) In boys, unfavourable neurological scores relate to a low level of play activity in the Blocks and Onetoy conditions, but to a relatively high level of play in the Vartoys condition. Such a difference is not found in the girls.

(3) Neurological dysfunctions contribute in a different manner to the neurobehavioural discrimination between boys and girls in the various conditions. Data which specify these relationships are summarized in Table 19.

TABLE 19
Neurological variables ranked according to their contribution to the distinction between neurobehavioural profiles.

	Neurol. sub-groups	Mo	Al 1	Al 2	Blocks	Vartoys	Onetoy	Sum of ranks
					Observation condition			
B	Posture	(1)	1	1	3	2	3	11
O	Sensorimotor	(2)	3	2	2	1	(4)	14
Y	Matur. responses	(4)	2	3	4	3	2	18
S	Choreiform mov.	(6)	4	(6)	1	(6)	1	24
	Co-ordination	(3)	5	(5)	(6)	4	(6)	29
	Matur. functions	(5)	(6)	(4)	5	(5)	(5)	30
G	Matur. functions	1	4	1	2	2	1	11
I	Sensorimotor	2	3	4	1	1	4	15
R	Co-ordination	4	1	2	4	5	2	18
L	Matur. responses	3	2	3	3	4	3	18
S	Posture	(5)	(6)	(5)	(6)	3	(6)	31
	Choreiform mov.	(6)	(5)	(6)	(5)	(6)	(5)	33

a) Rank numbers are based on analyses in which two profiles were determined.
b) Variables in parentheses do not contribute substantially to the discrimination between profiles.

These data show that:—

(a) in girls the categories 'sensorimotor', 'maturation of functions', 'maturation of responses' and 'co-ordination' contribute to the distinction between groups in all observation conditions. The categories 'posture' and 'choreiform movements' contribute little or nothing to the distinction between groups.

(b) In boys the categories 'posture', 'sensorimotor', and 'maturation of responses' contribute to the distinction between profiles in all conditions, while 'co-ordination' and 'maturation of functions' do not contribute to any of them.

(c) In boys there were some intriguing findings in relation to choreiform movements. This category has the lowest contribution of all neurological variables in four observation conditions, but the highest in the Blocks and Onetoy conditions. This may indicate that *choreiform dyskinesia specifically affects the organization of the boys' behaviour in conditions with a lack of variation in environmental stimuli.*

Intervening variables

Neurobehavioural profiles indicate how, in sub-groups of children, variables are related to each other. However, numerous factors may have affected the associations between neurological findings and behaviour: neurological and behavioural variables belong to a much larger complex of mutually dependent factors.

The effect of the sex differences has already been eliminated by the separate analysis in boys and girls. From the other possible intervening factors I traced back the effect of the socio-educational milieu (crudely estimated by the school education of the parents) and the age of the child.

No very complex statistical procedures were carried out with the social measures as these were not a main focus of this study. Undoubtedly, if analyses were carried out, significant findings would emerge. It is perhaps worth commenting that the difference in living conditions and physical circumstances are not as great in an area such as that around Groningen as they are some of the larger cities of the world such as New York, London or Amsterdam. A case selection too of children who were born in the hospital also affects the range of variation of social class within the sample.

Age

Significant age differences are only found between neurobehavioural groups in the girls in the condition 'with mother in the unfamiliar room' and in the boys in the Onetoy condition. In the novel room with mother, girls showing a high amount of exploratory activity are younger than those behaving more passively ($p = < .02$, Mann-Whitney U test, two-tailed). In the Onetoy condition younger boys are slightly over-represented in the groups with low neurological scores ($N = 17$, $N = 22$) as compared to one of the groups with favourable neurological scores ($N = 17$ versus $N = 12$, $p < .04$; $N = 22$ versus $N = 12$, $p < .02$).

Socio-educational milieu

Only in the boys in the Blocks condition do groups differ significantly as to the school education of the father and the mother. Both social background measures are higher for the group with high neurological scores (who play at a high level) than for the other group (p < .007 for school education mother, and p < .005 for school education father). Other differences do not reach significance, although trends are generally towards slightly higher school-training scores in the parents of children with higher neurological scores. This reflects the fact that neurological scores in this group have a slight relationship to socio-economic class.

CHAPTER 7

Discussion

In this chapter I am going to review some of the previous work which has been done on the relationship between neurological status and behaviour, but it is first necessary to disabuse the reader of any idea that neurological status is the only, or even the most important, determinant of variations in behaviour in children with minor nervous dysfunctions.

Brain and Behaviour

One of the striking findings in this study is how much the environment, and indeed quite minor changes in the environment, can alter the behaviour of young children, regardless of their neurological status. It might be supposed that children with severe neurological handicaps would show less variation in behaviour in different situations than would normal children (as indicated by the results of Hutt *et al.* 1965), but the present study emphasises that behavioural variation is to a large extent determined by the immediate environment. In our study of 117 children, only one child was in the population group with the highest amount of motor activity for all six observation conditions. This finding deserves some attention from those interested in hyperactivity, and also indicates that stereotyped opinions about neurobehavioural relationships are fallacious. This point is highly relevant for the later discussion of 'Minimal Brain Dysfunction'.

The implication is that even a mildly impaired system has a large amount of freedom to vary behaviour. This view of the variability of behaviour is very similar to that advanced by writers such as Waddington (1971), whose view of the genetic control of behaviour is far less restrictive than that of some earlier geneticists. Waddington's conception is of 'chreods' or 'pathways of development' which allow many factors to influence behaviour but do, nevertheless, put some genetic limitation on the organism's adaptability. Waddington postulates that there are genetically-based differences in the organism's capacity to maintain its functional integrity in the presence of external stress. Hence one may take Waddington's concept and use it to state that despite the neurological impairment the organism has a great deal of freedom and is able to display a wide variety of behaviours, but that it does imply some limits on the organism's ability to adapt. One should, therefore, be most careful in selecting educational environments for children with neurological impairment. Those environments which cause stress to the child will be most sensitive in distinguishing between children with and without neurological problems.

In the present study, the differences in behaviour between neurologically optimal and non-optimal children were more apparent in mildly distressing situations than in more stimulating situations. This shows that children with minor neurological disorders may function quite well in a moderately stimulating, but not too distracting, environment. This result throws some doubt on the view of some educationalists that children with neurological disorders function best in a dull unstimulating environment. However, much detailed observation will be necessary to define the optimal learning conditions for various categories of problem children.

Neither the genetic make-up nor the neurological status account to any very great extent for the variability in behaviour. From the very beginning of extra-uterine life there exists a complex interaction between the individual and his environment.

Certain behaviours of the infant may trigger specific reactions in the caretaker, and *vice versa*. For example, newborns who adapt their movements and body posture smoothly to those of the mother may give her less difficulty in handling than infants who are motorically inconsistent. So-called 'apathetics' possibly get less attention from parents than alert newborns who react spontanteously. Also, the initial reaction tendencies of the child may be strengthened by his social environment.

As the human newborn is studied more and more, precise observation of developing social interactions in groups of children of varying biological and neurological make-up will be needed in order to reach a better understanding of the determination of behavioural differences. Clearly, behavioural differences between children at pre-school age have at least partly developed as a result of such complex interactions. (See Chapter 6).

Animal Studies

Experimental studies in animals have shown that the effects of gross brain damage are, to quite a large extent, situation-bound. Thomson *et al.* (1969) studied adult Rhesus monkeys who had had bilateral amygdalectomies in infancy. They observed that, on introduction to a new situation, the experimental monkeys shifted more rapidly from one behaviour to another than did the controls. (This is perhaps suggestive of stress.) This difference was only observed during the first few hours, however, and after 24 hours there were no differences between experimental monkeys and controls in respect of this behaviour. When the animals were settled in, Thomson also observed that they differed in the way they explored: the experimental monkeys showed more exploratory behaviour, particularly of an oral and manipulative kind, than the controls.

Bowden *et al.* (1971) studied Rhesus monkeys who had had surgery bilaterally in the pre-frontal cortex, and again followed the monkeys through to adult life. They found strong differences in the way the experimental animals and control group behaved in social and non-social situations. While the experimental monkeys tended to sleep more than the controls in social situations, they were more active than the controls when isolated. In his discussion Bowden suggests that the situation plays a large part in modulating the arousal mechanisms of the brain.

Animal studies also show that brain impairment does not necessarily lead to lower performance. Animals with specific brain lesions learn more rapidly in certain circumstances than undamaged animals. Johnson (1972) reports that rats with septal lesions learned avoidance tasks more quickly than normal controls, and Musty (1969) reports that rats with hippocampal lesions press levers in a learning task at a higher rate than controls. It is possible that disinhibition occurs in the brain-damaged animals, with the result that simple isolated tasks can be performed quite well, but performance in complex tasks is disturbed. However, this does not explain the fact that the children in our study with poor neurological status performed better than those with good neurological status. In this case, the most important factors affecting behaviour in unstimulating situations seem to be differences in motivation and in the capacity for sustained attention.

Windle's (1969) many studies show that quite large and substantial early brain damage may have very little effect on adult functioning of monkeys. His findings give support to the views of people such as Benton (1973) who believe that children with quite minor functional difficulties may have relatively large areas of brain damage.

Experimental studies in rats by Schwartz (1964) show how environmental and neurological factors can interact in behavioural development. Rats with and without neonatal cortical lesions were raised to early adulthood in environments that afforded either minimal or maximal opportunity for perceptual and motor experience. Behavioural testing in adults showed that both brain damage and the quality of the environment alone can affect the performance on a maze learning test, but that there is also an interaction between these variables. The negative effects of neonatal lesions on adult behaviour were significantly offset by an enriched early environment.

Of course, these studies of animals must be interpreted with great care in relation to human behaviour.

Results of the Present Study Compared with Previous Work—Reactions to Novelty

In the present study different reactions to novelty were observed in children with low and high neurological scores. Especially in girls, unfavourable neurological scores are often associated with a high amount of room exploration when the child is alone with the mother, while girls with more favourable scores show signs of discomfort and keep close to the mother.

An exaggeration of exploratory activity was also observed by Corinne Hutt (1968) in severely brain-damaged pre-school children on first exposure to novel objects.

Vinogradova (1961), quoted by Stores (1973), reports an exaggeration and diminution of the orientation response in relation to brain damage in humans, while Rosner (1970) concludes, in a review of the pertinent research, that 'brain injury may disrupt normal control over reactions to novel stimuli'. Evidence comes mainly from animal studies such as those by Kimble *et al.* (1967). Kimble reports that hippocampal (but not cortical) lesions lead to an increase in exploratory behaviour in rats.

Luria also reports that humans with lesions in the pre-frontal cortex over-react to novel stimuli (Luria 1973). Such lesions may lead to marked disinhibition of immediate responses to irrelevant stimuli, thus making the performance of complex behavioural programmes impossible.

Hutt and Hutt (1964) indicate that as a consequence of an exaggeration of inspective activity, other, more creative behaviours do not develop. Slotnick (1967) reports that female rats subjected to early cingulate lesions did poorly in retrieving and nursing their young in a strange environment, but not in a familiar one.

It seems far-fetched to relate findings in our relatively normal pre-school children to those in animals with experimental brain lesions and to those in children with severe brain damage. However, there is growing evidence, from animal studies and clinical observation of humans, that severe brain lesions acquired in early infancy

87

may result in only minor dysfunction at later ages. Nevertheless, it seems unjustified to conclude, on the basis of these analogies, that the high amount of exploration in the pre-school girls with low neurological scores indicates brain damage.

Girls with favourable neurological scores in our pre-school group showed more inhibitory reactions in the unfamiliar room, keeping close to the mother and looking around before exploring the room further. Similar observations have been reported by Hutt *et al.* (1965) on normal controls. The children surveyed the environment before exploring or playing. The active exploration would be interrupted by brief periods of simply looking around. The brain-damaged children did not show this apprehensive reaction, but started moving around immediately. Unfortunately, Hutt *et al.* do not report results for boys and girls separately.

On the basis of the view that negative reactions to strangeness increase with age, Hutt *et al.* considered the behaviour of the brain-damaged children as comparable to that in normal children of a younger age.

In our study, the girls who explored were younger than those who did not, which may suggest an interaction between neurological condition and age in the determination of the amount of exploratory behaviour in girls. However, no relationship between exploratory behaviour and age was found in the boys. More information is yet needed to substantiate the relationship between brain dysfunction and amount of exploratory activity in relation to age.

Although the children with unfavourable neurological scores in our study initially explored more than those with favourable scores, in subsequent observation conditions their exploration dropped to a level below that seen in the children with favourable neurological scores. It seems, therefore, that children with unfavourable scores need more stimulation to remain interested in the environment.

Interestingly enough, the boys with low neurological scores maintained a high level of exploration after the initial condition, but the girls with low scores dropped to an exploration level below that of the girls with favourable scores.

This rapid decrease in exploratory activity in children with unfavourable neurological scores is in contrast to the slow 'habituation' of brain-damaged children reported by Hutt *et al.* (1965) and Hutt (1968). They attribute the phenomenon to the 'short-sampling' tendency in the brain-damaged subjects. The slow habituation seems to be an aspect of the 'invariability' which Hutt *et al.* find in the brain-damaged group. This phenomenon is perhaps directly linked to cognitive deficits which make the brain-damaged children incapable of modulating their behaviour in response to environmental change.

In this study, satiation reactions were observed in children with unfavourable neurological scores in the Alone 1 and Alone 2 conditions, which suggests that a loss of interest in the environment is a prominent factor. This rapid loss of interest after an initial peak of activity is often reported by teachers of children with learning disorders. Sykes *et al.* (1973) have described this phenomenon in hyperactive children who were unable to maintain attention over a prolonged period of time. These children were described as appearing to lack inhibitory control and showing more impulsive reactions to novel stimuli. Luria (1973) mentions this as an inability to modulate activity, frequently found in relation to damage of the pre-frontal cortex. Close observation of behaviour in free-field settings may reveal such reaction tendencies in neurologically impaired pre-school children.

As yet, no satisfactory explanation (in terms of brain processes) has been given for this high initial exploratory activity. Berlyne (1960) describes the function of exploratory activity as 'maintaining a balance between internal factors and incoming stimulation'. Hutt *et al.* (1965) suggest that an individual has an optimal level of stimulation (arousal potential) which is considered 'a state of the reticular activating system'. Novel, complex and uncertain stimuli increase internal arousal and the animal seeks to reduce this by specific inspective exploration.

When the level of stimulation is too low, arousal may occur as cortical restraints upon the reticular system are released. This may give rise to diversive exploration which serves to vary sensory input, *e.g.* body-oriented activity or room-oriented activity.

Such an arousal model seems to be a physiological pseudo-explanation: 'arousal' is used in the sense of a 'tendency to react', with no independent evidence of the physiological mechanisms involved. It seems, in a circular way, to redescribe the exploratory activity that has been observed.

Play Behaviour

Play behaviour shows interesting differences in relation to neurological scores. Girls with unfavourable scores play at low levels and so do boys. The exception for the boys is the Vartoys condition. This condition was chosen to investigate problems of selective attention. The child is confronted with a large variety of toys, in contrast to the Blocks condition. Of all the toys, the boys found the constructive material most attractive. The attractiveness of the toys is especially important for children with neurological dysfunction; these children are described by their parents as easily distracted and bored unless very attractive play material is offered to them.

The difference in play behaviour between boys and girls in the Vartoys condition may possibly be explained by the fact that the Vartoys condition was less attractive to the girls. This raises the general problem in studying boys and girls in identical situations, that the objective similarity of the environment may obscure the subjective difference for the two sexes. Girls with low neurological scores may function better in conditions more suited to them.

Whatever the correct explanation may be, these results indicate at least that consequences of neurological impairment manifest themselves differently in different environments. The behavioural sequelae of an unfavourable neurological condition appears most clearly in situations with an element of uncertainty, sensory deprivation, or strangeness.

A striking feature in the studies of Hutt *et al.* (1965) was the invariability of the duration and range of activities in the brain-damaged group. The group was affected very little by changes in the structure of the environment. Another study by Hutt *et al.* (1965) showed the same invariability in hyperactive children.

An equally striking feature of my data is the large variability in neurobehavioural relationships. If, for instance, the boys with low and high (favourable and unfavourable) neurological scores had only been observed in the unfamiliar room with their mothers, hardly any difference in behaviour would have been spotted. In the Alone 1 condition the boys with low scores are the explorers, but these same boys behave most passively in the Alone 2 condition. In the Blocks condition these boys show the lowest levels of play activity, but in the Vartoys condition they show the highest levels, and again the lowest level of play activity in the Onetoy condition. Only by careful description of context and behaviour can any meaningful data be obtained. Differences in neurobehavioural relationships relate not only to the features of that specific environment but also to the wider context in which observations are carried out.

The Concept of Minimal Brain Dysfunction (M.B.D.)

One of the most remarkable clinical concepts is that of M.B.D., originally termed 'minimal brain damage', at present 'minimal brain dysfunction'. The term is generally used to identify school-aged children of normal intelligence, who present behaviour and/or learning problems which are assumed to be connected with minimal C.N.S. dysfunction. Terms such as over- or hyperactivity, short attention span and lack of concentration, impulsivity, lability of mood, and irritability purport to describe disorders in behavioural organisation, frequently observed in such children, while deficits in the perception and integration of spatial and temporal relationships are also often reported, usually in connection with reading and/or writing difficulties. 'Soft' neurological signs, such as minor deficiencies in motor co-ordination, reflex asymmetries, mild visual or hearing impairments, dyskinesia (such as choreiform jerks, athetoid movements), general clumsiness, poor fine or gross visuo-motor co-ordination, and signs of a delayed motor development are also frequently part of the syndrome.

The fact that many authors all use these terms reflects a wide-spread belief in the M.B.D. stereotype rather than a reliable and valid bulk of research studies demonstrating that such children exist. Many of these descriptions are based on terminology used by writers such as Ounsted to describe children with unequivocal evidence of brain damaged (Ounsted 1955). Few problem areas have evoked as much interest in specialists of such widely varying disciplines as physics, psychology, education and biochemistry, as the M.B.D. syndrome. At the same time, however, hardly any concept in the clinical nomenclature has occasioned so much controversy and confusion. What has led to this broad interest and what is the background of the confusion and controversy?

The growing complexity of scholastic standards, the refinement in diagnostic tools and the development of institutions for special education led to the identification of groups of children with learning problems, previously unrecognised or not manifesting themselves. Strongly influenced by Piaget, there was a growing knowledge and recognition of the essential rôle of the child's 'organismic make-up' in the development of his adaptation to the social and physical environment. Specific learning problems were attributed to basic defects in the integration of motor and perceptual information.

There was a considerable change in neuropsychological thinking, which evolved from the previous mechanistic connectionist models to the idea that the nervous system functions as a differentiated whole in continuous interaction with the environment (Boring 1960). Contemporary neuropsychological thinking, as exemplified by

Luria (1973), considers the C.N.S. as a totally active, integrated system, responsible for the refined adaptation of the behaviour to environmental variations. Diffuse damage to the cerebrum may lead to disorders in the organisation of complex behaviour, such as those described in so-called M.B.D. children.

In clinical thinking, descriptions of phenomena associated with demonstrable brain pathology in adults have had a strong effect on thinking about developmental disturbances. The aphasia literature in particular, focussing attention on disorders in receptive and expressive language in relation to brain disorder has affected the development of the M.B.D. concept. Disorders in the acquisition of spoken and written language become considered as analogues of such aphasic phenomena in adults (Strother 1973). When hard evidence for brain damage is lacking in children presenting such developmental disorders, the label 'M.B.D.' is generally used to suggest the organic background.

A similar development occurred in connection with other phenomena related to adult brain pathology, such as functional retrogression and loss of abstract reasoning ability. By analogy, developmental delays and persistent concrete modes of thinking also became considered as signs of C.N.S. disorder, although it was realised that developmental disorders were different from signs of functional disintegration in brain-damaged adults.

Another important influence on the development of the M.B.D. concept has been descriptions of the behavioural consequences of known brain damage in children. After encephalitis (Hohman 1922, Bond 1932) and after head injuries (Strecker and Ebaugh 1924, Blau 1936) behavioural disorders have been reported with symptoms such as lack of motor inhibition, extreme unselectivity in attention, emotional lability, irritability, often without intellectual impairment.

The concept of a 'continuum of degrees of damage' led to the view that minor C.N.S. disorders would be likely to manifest themselves in the disorganisation of the child's complex behaviour, even in the absence of unequivocal neurological signs (see Strother 1973). Etiological studies (initially retrospective, later also prospective), indicating relationships between complex behaviour disorders of the M.B.D. type and risk factors early in development, gave some indirect support to this view. Such finding, however, don't justify the reversed reasoning that behaviour disorders in themselves are sufficient evidence for brain damage or brain dysfunction. Strauss and associates are generally held responsible for the introduction of this sort of reasoning. They initially identified a number of psychological characteristics distinguishing brain-injured from non brain-injured mentally retarded children (Strauss and Kephart 1940, Strauss and Lehtinen 1947), whereas they later assume that the presence of such characteristics in themselves indicates brain damage.

These various developments all contributed to the view of minimal brain damage as a primary causative factor in the development of complex learning and/or behaviour disorders in children. Replacement of the term 'minimal brain damage' by 'minimal brain dysfunction' was more an indication of modesty than a contribution to the insight in the problem of neurobehavioural connections in children. In this respect the Oxford conference in 1962 was important (Bax and Mac Keith 1963). Participants agreed that the term 'minimal brain damage' should be abandoned, because of lack of evidence that structural defects formed the basis for the behavioural disorders the group was discussing. No agreement was reached, however, about another term to cover this heterogeneous group of children. The editors issued the proceedings of the meeting under the title of 'Minimal Cerebral Dysfunction'. This label together with 'minimal brain dysfunction' replaced the earlier tag of 'minimal brain damage'.

What is the present state of knowledge and what seems to be the most fruitful approach in the study of neurobehavioural relationships in children?

Valid Findings

Signs of neurological dysfunction (including EEG abnormalities) are found consistently more often in children presenting learning and/or behaviour disorders of the M.B.D. type than in matched controls (Schain 1970, Hughes 1971, Satterfield *et al.* 1971, Werry 1972, Myklebust 1973). Children are termed hyperactives, under-achievers, M.B.D. cases, *etc.*; the neurological concomitants include soft signs, unspecified EEG disorders, longer latency and lower amplitude evoked cortical responses, *etc.* An excellent review of the evidence is given by Walzer and Richmond (1973). More signs of neurological dysfunction have also been found in delinquent boys and blind children than in normal children (Wolff and Hurwitz 1966).

In a large number of epidemiological studies complex learning and behaviour disorders of the M.B.D. type have been reported as sequelae of pre- and perinatal complications, such as anoxia and hypoxia (Rosenfeld and Bradley 1948, Fraser and Wilks 1959, Schachter and Apgar 1959, Knoblock and Pasamanick 1966) pre-maturity or dysmaturity (Knobloch *et al.* 1956) toxic factors, such as lead poisoning (Mellins and Jenkins 1955) and infective diseases (Hohman 1922, Lurie and Levy 1942), and malnutrition in infancy (Richardson *et al.* 1973), suggesting a neurological basis for such disorders. However, outcomes of various studies are far from unequivocal, partly due to methodological differences (Gottfried 1973).

To date there is only one study which demonstrated behavioural differences between groups distinguished solely on the bases of neurological dysfunctions. This is the study by Wolff and Hurwitz (1973), in which children with choreiform dyskinesia received less favourable behavioural ratings from teachers than non-choreiforms. Rutter *et al.* (1966) failed to find such associations. There is thus a lack of experimental studies, but no shortage of clinical impressionistic articles in the area of Minimal Brain Dysfunction (Zimet and Fishman 1970). This has been extensively discussed in a previous survey (Kalverboer 1971c).

By far the best clinical neuropsychiatric study into the significance of brain disorders for behavioural development is that by Rutter *et al.* reported in *A Neuropsychiatric Study in Childhood* (1970). However, they focus on psychiatric characteristics of children with cerebral palsy, epilepsy, and a number of other unequivocal pathological conditions. They refrain from studying the group of less well-defined, borderline neurological disorders, which are just those disorders typically reported in relation to the M.B.D. concept.

As far as objective measurement of behaviour is concerned, one of the best studies is that by Schulman *et al.* (1965) on relationships between behavioural, psycho-metric and neurological measures in a group of 35 retarded boys. They applied a number of objective measures for the evaluation of behavioural aspects, such as inconsistency, distractability, hyperactivity and emotional lability. However, they relate their behavioural findings to global ratings of brain damage derived from psychometric tests (Wechsler), EEGs, and neurological examinations, the validity of which, as indicators of brain damage, may be seriously questioned. Schulman is by no means the worst offender in using subjective and arbitrary measures. Similar usage, employing such terms as 'organicity', 'brain damage', and 'brain dysfunction', can be found in recent literature, (e.g. Sainz 1966, Paine 1968, Wender 1971). Birch (1964) suggests that 'medical and psychological examiners tend to use one another as the essential independent proof of the validity of their inferences'. Birch illustrates this with the story of the artillery sergeant and the clock-maker, each of them proving that he is right by referring to the other.*

Written in 1963, this statement still largely holds. Often it is impossible to obtain a direct and unequivocal proof of brain damage, or brain dysfunction. Birch and Demb (1953) point out that, as a result, the clinical diagnosis of brain damage in children with adjustment problems is made more often than not on essentially behavioural grounds.

Benton (1962) argues that many studies, intended to disclose the relationship between organism and response, only reflect that between response and response. In the words of Benton: 'they relate characteristics of psychological test performance to behavioural characteristics as clinically observed'. Although it may be very useful to establish such relationships, they don't tell us anything about the consequences of brain damage, because an independent criterium for brain damage is lacking.

Conclusions

What conclusion can be drawn from a study of the available literature? Terms such as M.B.D. (minimal brain dysfunction) and S.L.D. (special learning disorders) refer to a group of children heterogeneous with respect to the disorders they present and the possible etiology of their adaptational problems.

Gomez (1967) considered the introduction of a diagnostic label such as 'Minimal Cerebral Dysfunction' as a backward step in the nosology of disorders of behaviour and learning, and pleaded for more descriptive sub-classifications. He argued for refraining from the use of such labels in an article entitled 'Minimum Cerebral Dysfunction, Maximum Neurological Confusion'.

---

*Many years ago a visitor to a small garrison town was impressed by the fact that each evening, at the stroke of five, the artillery sergeant lowered the colours and ordered his squad to fire a cannon. Amazed at such punctuality, the visitor enquired of the sergeant as to how he determined when it was precisely five o'clock. The sergeant replied that the town was famous not only for the excellence of its garrison but because one of its inhabitants was perhaps the best clock-maker in the world. 'Each morning', he said, 'as I walk past the clock-maker's shop I re-set my own watch and therefore know that when I fire the cannon it is precisely five o'clock'. Only partially satisfied by this answer, the visitor went into town and addressed himself to the clock-maker, saying 'Sir, could you please tell me how you achieved your reputation for having clocks that are always precisely on time?' The clock-maker replied, 'Well, living in this town I have a special advantage. You see, every evening precisely at five o'clock the garrison gun goes off and I re-set all my clocks at that time'.

Some people have suggested using more descriptive terms, such as 'delayed or irregular maturation' (Abrams 1968). However, as stated by Dinnage (1970), 'whatever term is used, it refers to a mixed group of handicaps with no known organic basis'.

There is no scientific evidence linking behavioural disorders and independent signs of neurological dysfunction in children which would justify including them all in one 'minimal brain dysfunction syndrome' (Schulman *et al.* 1965, Rutter *et al.* 1966, Werry 1968). Even the relationships among the behavioural features themselves seem to be much weaker than is generally assumed (Routh and Roberts 1972). Often such relationships seem to depend more on the perceptual and cognitive schemata of the observer than on the factual behaviour of the child.

Many M.B.D. studies show fallacies, such as the following:
(a) Biased groups, often groups of children referred to outpatient clinics because of behavioural and/or learning disorders.
(b) Dubious criteria for brain damage or brain dysfunction.
(c) Lack of standardisation of methods for neurological and behavioural assessment.
(d) Built-in correlations between data from different assessments.
(e) Relating poorly-defined so-called 'soft' neurological signs to complex behaviour disorders.

Clinical descriptions and psychometric data almost exclusively concern school-aged children presenting learning and behavioural problems. Data are lacking relating children's free-field behaviour to their neurological condition, although problems reported by parents often concern daily life adaptation. The study of young children (preferably before school-age), not selected because of their adaptational problems but on the basis of their neurological make-up, may be particularly fruitful.

In the light of the above discussion, the best strategy in M.B.D. studies in children seems to be to analyse in detail the behavioural repertoire in relevant situations and to relate findings to those obtained in comprehensive neurological assessments. This is what this study attempts to do.

Relevance of the present study

It is important to stress that a label such as M.B.D. cannot be applied to most children described in this study. The M.B.D. concept is traditionally linked to the school-age (approx. 7 to 12), involving learning and concentration difficulties, usually not yet present in that form at pre-school age. Only a few of the children in this follow-up sample presented adaptational problems of the M.B.D. type. No child was included in the sample because of the existence of such difficulties. (Detailed selection criteria are given in Chapter 2.)

However, the findings in this study may throw some light on relationships between neurological signs and behaviour. In this group such relationships have not yet been obscured by 'secondary' effects due to the child's interaction with his social environment, which may have strengthened the original problem behaviour. This is often the case in clinical studies of children referred to a hospital because of maladaptive behaviour. Phenomena such as 'hyperpaedophilia' (Ounsted 1955) and 'the self-perpetuating cycle' (Eisenberg 1957) refer to such factors.

In our study there is only a weak link between the neurological status and the behaviour. Differences in neurological status account for no more than five per cent of the variance in the free-field behaviour. There are large numbers of children with unfavourable status who deviate from the general relationships described in the study. This implies that detailed behavioural assessments are necessary in young children suspected of being at risk for developing neurobehavioural problems.

However, there are substantial relationships demonstrated in this study. Problems in the organisation of the behaviour related to the child's neurological status are most frequently observed in situations with unattractive material. Children with some neurological impairment are, even more than others, in need of a stimulating and varied learning environment! However, the situation should be carefully designed. Behavioural observations may be of considerable help in defining the most suitable environment for the child.

The contribution of neurological categories to the discrimination between groups is more complex than suggested by the crude distinction between high and low neurological scores. These complexities are displayed in two ways: (1) different neurological conditions are important for the behaviour in boys and girls (Table 18), (2) different neurological conditions have different relationships to behaviour in different environments. The manner in which choreiform dyskinesia in particular affects the behavioural organisation strongly depends on the environment.

In preliminary analyses, a much stronger connection between neurological findings and behaviour was found in boys than in girls. However, in the final profile analysis connections are about equally strong in both sexes. This is mainly due to the addition of the categories 'maturation of functions' and 'maturation of responses'. These categories contribute strongly to the discrimination in the girls, but little in the boys, while on the other hand 'choreiform movements' have an effect on behaviour in boys only. Although no conclusions about M.B.D. can be drawn from these data, one might speculate that Kinsbourne's (1973) view that 'all indicators of M.B.D. represent the normal state of affairs in younger children' does not equally hold for boys and girls. In girls the dysmaturity aspect may be predominant, whereas in boys the aspect of neurological dysfunction may play a more prominent rôle in the genesis of the typical M.B.D. case. As learning and behavioural problems of the M.B.D. type are much more common in boys than in girls, one might speculate that at school-age, the dysfunctions of the C.N.S. are more important in the determination of such difficulties than dysmaturity of the C.N.S.

This view is strongly supported by my results. A particular example is the specific association between choreiform movements and free-field behaviour in boys. This neurological condition exists in low-level play with unattractive toys, but fails to show up in all other examined conditions. Its specificity is also indicated in our group by the lack of correlations between choreiform movements and other neurological conditions. Choreiform dyskinesia has to be considered as a dysfunction of the C.N.S. (Touwen and Prechtl 1970) but not as a sign of developmental delay (highest frequency found is 12 per cent in boys at seven years of age (Stemmer 1964)). Much of the controversy around choreiform dyskinesia (Prechtl and Stemmer 1962, Rutter et al. 1966, Wolff and Hurwitz 1966, Nooteboom 1967) can be explained by this specific connection to adaptive behaviour in boys which differs from that of other neurological conditions.

This study clearly shows that it does not make any sense to describe the child's neurological status in terms of undiscriminated 'soft signs'.

Much further study of neurobehavioural relationships is needed. Both neurological and behavioural assessments are to a large extent concerned with behavioural functions or performances of the child. How such performances relate to structural properties of the brain or to brain processes is largely unknown. This should be considered when talking about 'neurobehavioural' relationships. On the one hand, difficulties in both areas may be manifestations of some underlying (neurological) disorder affecting the functional organisation in all its facets: on the other hand difficulties in the behavioural area may be a secondary effect of minor neurological dysfunctions, *e.g.* the presence of neurological dysfunction such as dyskinesia may prevent the child from performing complex activities smoothly and efficiently, such as writing, building with blocks, *etc.*

Results of this study support the first sort of explanation. However, systematic and close follow-up studies, starting early in development, are necessary to detect more precisely the background of these neurobehavioural relationships. Our results can help in formulating hypotheses to be tested in such studies.

Validity for Daily Life Situations

Various follow-up studies of the children in the present study are in progress in which we have collected data about school performance (at the age of eight and nine) and, of course, we initially had questionnaire data both from the kindergarten teachers and the children's parents. Some analysis of these data has already been made and one immediate problem that arises is that the reports by mothers and teachers and the observations of the neurologist and the psychologist about the children's activities correlate rather poorly. It is not surprising therfore that on first glance the correlations between reported behaviours and free-field measures are poor. The next step is clearly to make actual observations in the home and school situation with some objective recording and see how these compare with the measures we have developed in the free-field laboratory situation.

Another subsidiary study we have carried out suggests that the parents' and teachers' reports of hyperactivity correlate less with the total amount of locomotion but more with consistency, so that children who are quiet for periods of time but then suddenly display a lot of locomotor activity are described as over-active, in contrast to children who have steady rates of relatively high or low activity. This result is in agreement with those of other investigators, such as Schulman *et al.* (1965).

However, the results of all these investigations simply confirm what I stated at the outset in the Introduction: that generalisations about the child's behaviour from one situation to another are very dangerous to make and that therefore one has to be very cautious in one's clinical interpretation even if data are obtained as systematically as those reported here.

If correlations between descriptions of daily life behaviour and observations made in the laboratory are poor, it is not surprising that predictions from laboratory studies are hard to make. We have collected information on eight-year-olds from teachers and have asked them to assess our children in terms of their over-all class-room competence, and also asked them to look and report on their task-orientation. There are in fact some correlations between the neurobehavioural groups at five and eight years of age. The results are all in the expected direction but this finding, though gratifying of course, does not allow one to make any predictions about individual children.

Relationships of this material to obstetrical and neonatal data

In Chapter 1, I briefly mentioned the obstetrical and neonatal data which were available on these children. I have not reported here fully the results of analyses comparing the findings at five years to this earlier data.

As the neurological status at five years of age only accounts for 4 to 8 per cent of the variance in behaviour, it would be very surprising if there were high correlations between the neurological status in the newborn period and behaviour at five. Touwen (1971) has already reported on the correlations between neurological optimality scores in the neonatal period and at five years of age.

The correlations here were not significant and the only significant correlation was in boys who suffered no interval complications between the two diagnostic assessments (such as head traumas, meningitis, encephalitis, *etc.*). However, the correlation was not higher than .28 (p = .03) and not, therefore, useful for any individual prognosis.

In this study in five-year-olds, correlations between neonatal and follow-up neurological data were low compared to findings in previous follow-up studies by Dijkstra (1960) on children between 18 months and 3½ years of age and by Touwen (1971) on four-year-olds. The decrease in the correlation can be attributed partly to the longer period between neonatal and follow-up neurological examinations and partly to changes in obstetrical practice, such as a decline in the number of instrument deliveries between our first follow-up studies and this last one. These interventions in particular may have led to minor neurological disorders. The loss of this group reduced the variance of neonatal optimality scores, a factor that has a lowering effect on correlation coefficients.

Undoubtedly, correlations would have been much higher in a group with a higher risk of brain damage (Knobloch and Pasamanick 1963). The application, in our analysis, of 'over-all optimality scores' may also have obscured relationships between *specific* neurological and behavioural measures at early and later ages.

I have described elsewhere (Kalverboer *et al.* 1973) the relationships between the hyperexcitable and the apathetic syndromes in the newborn period (Prechtl and Beintema 1964) and free-field behaviour at age five. There were some meaningful correlations. The apathetic group showed less exploratory behaviour and more contact with the mother in the first observation situation, and slightly more signs of distress, such as body manipulation in other empty room conditions. The hyperexcitable children were, surprisingly enough, functioning at slightly higher levels than optimal controls in the Onetoy situation. This, incidentally, was confirmed by rather better teacher reports on hyperexcitable children at eight, than the optimal controls in relation to the children's task orientation. This indicates that the significance of the hyperexcitability syndrome itself in the newborn period and its

97

relationship to later findings needs further careful study. We have also looked for relationships between the behavioural findings at five and the obstetrical data. No meaningful relationships were found.

Clinical applications of these methods

All these findings suggest that at the moment direct observation studies can at best provide one with a descriptive account of the child's functioning and distinguish between different neurological groups at the age at which the child is selected for study. They also may have very substantial value in assessing the effects of any therapeutic intervention, such as a drugs treatment programme, when serial observation may make it possible to estimate the efficacy of the treatment programme. Now that our technique has been established, it has (with no modification) many applications for the study of the behaviour of neurologically-impaired children, and for other clinical groups such as autistic or hearing-impaired children. As mentioned in Chapter 1, studies are now going on and will be reported elsewhere.

As a research tool, the method of free-field observation will obviously be suitable for developmental studies and for the study of children in longitudinal projects. Clinically, the method can be developed by selection from the present information of those situations and behaviour patterns which discriminate most clearly between different groups of children. The present study, focussing on children with some neurological impairment, suggests that measures of inconsistency in motor activity and in play level and of exploratory activity in new situations are probably the most sensitive behavioural items to look at in discriminating between these groups of children. Were one wishing to look at other differences, such as differences between boys and girls, one might select different behaviours and environments. The adaptation to the novel situation is a particularly sensitive discriminator here and mildly frustrating or boring situations also serve to discriminate between them. Again, therefore, if one wanted to study sex differences in behaviour, useful leads have emerged.

Psychologists in the past have looked in a very sophisticated way at the final output of a whole series of complex behaviour; that is to say, they have studied the results of the child's performance on a specific task and expressed them in quantitative scores. They have not, however, usually analysed the precise ways in which different children carry out different tasks, and it is probably this failure which has been at the root of the difficulties many psychologists have had in providing help either for teachers of normal or abnormal children when they get into trouble at school. This partly accounts for the difficulty in relating outcomes of such assessments to neurological findings, which may have much more to do with the way children and adults structure and organise their behaviour than with the end results. It is likely that these behaviours which one studies, rather than their end results, will be closely connected to neurological status, because a neurological examination is to a large extent a detailed observation of behaviour.

Another feature of the analysis which has been done here is to demonstrate the importance of selecting suitable tools for analysing very large amounts of data in clinical studies. Simple correlations can hardly give any useful information, and the application of a method such as profile analysis, which allows one to pick out some sub-groups, seems to us important. It does seem to suggest that given such types of analysis on the large and heterogeneous group of children presently bundled into the M.B.D. package, one might be able to sort out some realistic sub-groups and then really begin to follow up and find out how these children develop and investigate how they can best be helped.

Individual behaviour

The enormous variety of individual behaviour in these four- and five-year-olds, even in rather specific situations, is one of the striking findings of this study. Only one child showed consistency on such a simple measure as gross motor activity in all six situations, and variety, therefore, was the main finding.

The large variety points to the very complex determination of behavioural differences and suggests that expectations of rather uniform behaviour by children in environments such as schools are very mistaken. It emphasises the danger of describing children who fail to produce stereotyped and expected behaviour in these situations as abnormal, and suggests that linking any behaviour directly to an implication of brain damage is dangerous and unrealistic. One must define precisely the situation in which a child shows a particular behaviour and describe the behaviour meticulously before one attempts to speculate about the function of this behaviour and its relationship to any other phenomenon such as a child's neurological status.

APPENDICES

APPENDIX I

Optimality ranges for the items of the neurological optimality score at pre-school age*

Test	Optimal Response
active power	moderately strong
resistance to passive movements	moderately strong resistance
range of movements	full range without overstretch
muscle consistency	moderate
clasp-knife phenomenon	absent
cog-wheel phenomenon	absent
circumference of arms and legs	symmetrical
tendon reflexes of the legs	moderate
threshold of tendon reflexes of the legs	medium
tendon reflexes of the arms	moderate
threshold of the tendon reflexes of the arms	medium
abnormal skin reflex	evident contraction on both sides
plantar response	plantar flexion or no reaction
other skin reflexes of the leg on the toes	absent
glabella reflex	symmetrical brisk closing of the eyes
foot posture, sitting	symmetrical in median position
posture of the arms in forward extension	symmetrical without deviations from median or horizontal line
posture of the trunk, standing	symmetrical and straight
arm posture (standing)	symmetrical, hands median
leg posture (standing)	straight, symmetrical
foot posture (standing)	symmetrical arches median position
posture during walking	asymmetrical, body straight
ability to sit	possible without support
ability to stand	possible without support
walking	smooth and similar movements of trunk, legs and arms
following an object with eyes, head and trunk, sitting	balance without support of hands
response to push, sitting	balance without support of hands
response to push, standing	balance without change of foot position
kicking	adequate touching of examined hand in three positions
rebound	5cm
type of grasping of small object	pincer grasp
fingertip-nose test	adequate placing of the finger with eyes closed
Romberg test	standing still with no movement of feet
choreiform movements (distal, proximal)	absent
tremor	absent or slight high freq. tremor
choreathetosis	absent
facial musculature	symmetrical in rest and during mov.
pharyngeal arches	symmetrical in rest and during mov.
Chvosteks' response	absent
cornea reflex	brisk closing of the eyes
position of the eyes	centered
pursuit movements of the eyes	symmetrical, smooth
convergence	present and equal on both sides
optokinetic nystagmus	equal on both sides
directional nystagmus	grade 1 in 45° position of the eyes
visual fields	full range
pupillary reactions on light	directly and indirectly present
fundoscopy	well-outlined contours of papilla, no edema

*As listed by Touwen (1971). Details about scoring in: Touwen and Prechtl (1970): *The Neurological Examination of the Child with Nervous Dysfunction*. London: Spastics International Medical Publications with Heinemann Medical.

APPENDIX II

Video equipment

2 cameras, Philips EL 8010/02
  camera 1, zoom-lens Angenieux-Zoom type 10 × 15B; F.15 — 150 mm
  camera 2, wide angle lens: Canon C-16 33 mm 1:1.5
2 camera control units, Philips EL 8015/02
2 monitors, Philips EL 8100/03
1 Sync Pulse Generator, Philips EL 8250/01
1 video mixer, Philips EL 8255
        this mixer gives the possibility to switch from camera 1 to camera 2 (and back) in a smooth way
        without loosing synchronisation; it is also possible to give a mixed picture of both cameras
1 video recorder, Sony OV 120 — UE
        this recorder uses 2 inch wide videotape on which is 1 video track and 2 audio tracks
1 video monitor, Philips EL 8110/00/90 (large screen)

Audio equipment

1 microphone, Sennheiser
        this microphone is placed above the light diffuser in the middle of the room, not visible to the
        child
1 preamplifier, departmental design
        this device amplifies the signals from the microphone to a suitable level for sound input of the
        video recorder
1 audio amplifier Seloso Milano
        this amplifier is connected to a loudspeaker to monitor the sounds to be recorded and reproduced
        reproduced
1 time marker departmental design
        this time marker gives sound bursts in the following pattern:
        every 10 sec. a burst of 500 Hz (burst lasts about 1 sec., low tone)
        every minute a burst of 1000 Hz (burst lasts about 2 sec., high tone)

Protocol sheet for the scoring of video-recorded behaviour in empty room conditions

Name ....
Birth date ....
Date of obs. ....
Age

Condition: 0 with mother
0 alone, 1st time
0 alone, 2nd time

Duration .... min.

Case number ....
Observer ....

	10 sec epoch	locom.	loc. pat.	body post.	addit. mov.	manip. self.	manip. envir.	vis. fix.	vis. scan.	vocal mon. com.	other sounds	gestures
1	00											
2	10											
3	20											
4	30											
5	40											
6	50											
7	00											
8	10											
9	20											
10	30											
11	40											
12	50											

Instruction to the observer
Indicate in code which blocks are entered.
Indicate in code which locomotion patterns and body posture occur.
Indicate in code which fixtures and social figures are fixated or manipulated.

APPENDIX IIIB

Protocol sheet for the scoring of video-recorded behaviour in play conditions

Name .... Condition: 0 blocks + observer Case number ....
Birth date ....   0 variety of toys Observer ....
Date of obs. ....   0 one toy
Age .... Duration: .... min.

	10sec epoch	locom	loc patt.	body post.	addit. mov.	manip. self	manip. envir.	vis. fix.	vis. scann.	vocal comm.	play act.	play obj.	level act.	inact.
1	00													
2	10													
3	20													
4	30													
5	40													
6	50													
7	00													
8	10													
9	20													
10	30													
11	40													
12	50													

Instruction to the observer
Indicate in code which squares are entered.
Indicate in code which locomotion patterns and body postures occur.
Indicate in code which fixtures and social figures are fixated or manipulated.
Indicate in code which play activities occur and which toys are handled.

105

Reliability of the scoring of free-field behaviour from audio-video recordings [a]

Categories	Interscorer reliability			Score-rescore agreement			
	Pairs of scores	Double zeros	r*	Condition	Pairs of scores	Double zeros	r*
1 Locomotion	130	8	.99	pooled[c]	65	2	.99
Locomotion	30	2	.99	empty room			
2 Changes of body postures	130	6	.79	pooled	65	4	.92
Changes of body postures	30	3	.77	empty room			
3 Types of body postures	60	0	.87	pooled	23	0	.95
Types of body postures	30	0	.87	empty room			
4 Changes of locomotion patterns	130	11	.86	pooled	65	4	.92
Changes of locomotion patterns	30	0	.92	empty room			
5 Types of locomotion patterns	60	0	.84	pooled	23	0	.92
Types of locomotion patterns	30	0	.91	empty room			
6 Movements towards one-way screen	130	98	.90	pooled	65	14	.93
Movements towards one-way screen	30	4	.87	empty room			
7 Additional movements (discrete)	130	101	.82	pooled	65	17	.63
Additional movements (discrete)	30	14	.96	empty room			
8 Additional movements (contin.)	60	28	.82	pooled	23	11	.56
Additional movements (contin.)	30	16	.84	empty room			
9 Types of additional movements	60	36	.67	pooled	23	10	.62
Types of additional movements	30	14	.72	empty room			
10 Gestures	130	104	.80	pooled	65	50	.92
Gestures	30	17	.83	empty room			
11 Manipulation of fixtures	30	16	.83	play	23	11	.91
Manipulation of fixtures	30	6	.61	empty room			
12 Types of manip. fixtures	30	6	.43	empty room	11	5	.50
13 Manipulation of own body/clothes	60	8	.80	pooled	23	5	.84
Manipulation of own body/clothes	30	0	.82	empty room			
14 Visual fixation (nr)	130	70	.96	pooled	65	23	.97
Visual fixation (nr)	30	0	.87	empty room			
15 Looking around (= vis. scanning) (nr.)	130	72	.89	pooled	65	38	.87
Looking around (= vis. scanning) (nr.)	30	2	.83	empty room			
16 Looking straight ahead (nr.)	130	96	.83	pooled	65	48	.83
Looking straight ahead (nr.)	30	5	.72	empty room			

	Categories	Interscorer reliability				Score-rescore agreement		
		Pairs of scores	Double zeros	r*	Condition	Pairs of scores	Double zeros	r*
17	Sounds (non-verbal)	60	50	.88	pooled	23	17	.90
	Sounds (non-verbal)	30	26	.86	empty room	23	16	.71
18	Verbalisation	60	43	.74	pooled	—	—	—(b)
	Verbalisation	30	22	.96	empty room			
19	Crying	60	56	1.00	pooled	—	—	—(b)
20	Spatial contact Ch-M	10(30)(d)	0	.84(.91)	Mo	5(15)	0	(.82)(d)
21	Tactile contact Ch-M (discr.)	10(30)	2(9)	.90(.92)	Mo	5(15)	0(6)	(.72)
22	Tactile contact Ch-M (contin.)	10(30)	4(17)	.69(.74)	Mo	5(15)	1(3)	(.70)
23a	Visual contact Ch-M	10(30)	0(8)	.74(.89)	Mo	5(15)	0	(.76)
23b	Visual contact with mother or observer	39	5	.84	Mo	16	2	(.96)
24	Verbal contact with mother or observer	20	5	.89	Mo	8	0	—(b)
25	Tactile contact M-Ch	10(30)	5(18)	.75(.78)	Mo	—	—	—(b)
26	Verbal contact M-Ch	10(30)	6(20)	.90(.92)	Mo	—	—	—(b)
27	Play activity level I	100	45	.73	Play	40	19	.75
28	Play activity level II	100	18	.83	Play	40	6	.86
29	Play activity level IIE	100	24	.70	Play	40	14	.69
30	Play activity level III	100	6	.87	Play	40	2	.90
31	Play activity level IV	100	71	.91	Play	40	35	.99
32	Tidying up activity	100	82	.90	Play	40	36	.89
33	Changes in play activity	70	5	.83	Vartoys	28	1	.84
34	Nr. of manipulated toys	50	5	.82	Blocks+Vartoys	20	0	.73
35	Changes in level of play activity	100	17	.80	Play	40	12	.84
36	Types of manip. toys	10	0	.90	Vartoys	5	0	—(b)
37	Longest play activity (dur.)	17	0	.74	Vartoys	10	0	.88
38	Absence of play activity (nr.)	100	60	.81	Play	40	20	.84
	Absence of play activity (dur.)	100	60	.98	Play	40	20	.87

(a) Because there were no significant differences between mean values of any of the variables these values are not presented.

(b) Insufficient data available for reliability estimation.

(c) 'Pooled' indicates that reliability coefficients are based on three-minute scores from *all* six observation conditions.
'Empty' indicates that reliability coefficients are based on three-minute scores, obtained in 'empty room' conditions (alone or with mother).
'Play' indicates that reliability coefficients are based on three-minute scores, obtained in all three play conditions.
'Vartoys' is condition with variety of toys, 'Blocks' is condition with blocks.

(d) Numbers between parentheses refer to control reliability analyses based on 30 or 15 pairs of one-minute scores.

* Pearson product-moment correlation.

APPENDIX IV B

Reliability of the coding procedure (N=120)

Categories	Reliability coefficient			
	1st min.	*2nd min.*	*3rd min.*	*total period*
locomotion	.98	.96	.97	
changes in body postures	.96	.95	.91	
types of body postures				.86
changes of locomotion patterns	.95	.92	.94	
types of locomotion patterns				.94
movements towards one-way screen	.80	.79	.63	
additional movements (discrete)	.75	.74	.60	
additional movements (contin.)				.78
types of additional movements				.74
gestures	.85	.83	.85	
manipulation of fixtures	.94	.92	.96	
types of manipulated fixtures				.93
manipulation of body/clothes	.89	.93	.93	
visual fixations (nr)	.89	.92	.93	
looking around (= visual scanning) (nr)	.98	.96	.84	
looking straight ahead (nr)	.92	.98	.93	
sounds				.79
verbalisation	.94	.96	.95	
crying				.99
spatial contact child-mother	.87	.93	.94	
tactile contact child-mother	.86	.88	.86	
tactile contact child-mother (contin.)				.86
visual contact child-mother	.87	.96	.89	
visual contact with mother or observer	.92	.96	.90	
verbal contact with mother or observer	.90	.95	.95	
tactile contact mother-child	.95	.85	.89	
verbal contact mother-child	.90	.96	.94	

APPENDIX VA

Observation condition 'in empty, unfamiliar room with mother'

Behaviour categories	Mean	St. deviation	Skewness	Kurtosis
Locomotion	47.19	34.104	0.747	3.03
Changes in body post/mov. patt.	22.40	12.753	1.432	5.25
Visual fixation (nr.)	17.26	6.152	0.372	2.99
Manip. of fixtures	3,49	2.899	1.006	4.00
Visual fixation (dur.)	91.90	26.289	—0.268	2.61
Mov. towards one-way-screen	0.96	1.463	2.203	8.86
Looking straight forward	20.46	21.120	1.916	7.04
Manip. of body (clothes)	5.11	3.534	0.608	2.72
Additional mov. (contin.)	0.79	1.537	2.624	10.94
Visual scanning	18.27	17.321	2.413	14.82
Tactile cont. child-mother	2.52	3.502	2.160	8.06
Spatial cont. child-mother (shortest dist.)	33.01	12.161	2.948	22.74
Visual cont. child-mother	10.25	3.404	—0.159	2.54
Verbal cont. child-mother	7.55	5.489	—0.058	1.75
Crying	0.04	0.310	8.470	74.99

Observation condition 'with mother in empty, unfamiliar room'

Behaviour categories		Correlations*													
Locomotion	1														
Body post./locom. patt.		+34													
Visual fixations (nr.)		+48	+28												
Manipulation of fixt.		+24	+25	+36											
Visual fixations (dur.)	2	+31	+18	+30	+33										
Mov. one-way screen		+15	+16	+14	+21	+38									
Looking straight ahead (dur.)	3	−21	−03	−41	−22	−57	−08								
Manip. of body (clothes)		−33	−18	−17	−14	−32	−15	+39							
Addit. movements (contin.)		−27	−22	−30	−21	−29	−13	+34	+48						
Visual scanning (dur.)		−40	−14	−23	−23	−34	−24	+22	+20	+17					
Tact. cont. child-mother	4	−29	−21	−29	−27	−29	−09	+26	+26	+10	+24				
Spat. cont. child-mother		−22	−25	−37	−33	−37	−20	+24	+19	+08	+20	+49			
Visual cont. child-mother	5	+19	+22	+30	+02	−20	−08	−32	−17	−23	−16	−28	−18		
Verbal cont. child-mother	6	+01	+07	+08	+12	+18	+03	−13	−29	−17	−14	−07	−19	+04	
Crying		−09	−02	−09	−10	−11	−08	+17	+21	+17	−06	−02	+20	+06	−04	−04

*A number of categories were excluded from the over-all analysis for various reasons, such as experimental dependence, application in specific analyses, too low frequency of occurrence: this applies also to Appendices VIB to XB.

Behaviour patterns
1 room exploration
2 one-way screen reactions
3 passive waiting/body-oriented act.
4 close contact
5 visual contact
6 verbal contact

APPENDIX VIA

Observation condition 'first time alone in empty room'

Behaviour categories	Mean	St. deviation	Skewness	Kurtosis
Locomotion	42.63	43.157	2.060	8.38
Changes in body post/mov. patt.	14.14	8.006	1.037	5.68
Visual fixation (nr.)	15.49	5.999	0.645	2.96
Manip. of fixtures	4.63	3.604	0.742	2.98
Visual fix. (dur.)	145.88	29.668	−1.340	4.72
Mov. towards one-way-screen	2.85	3.000	1.277	4.76
Looking straight forward	18.96	19.789	1.606	5.64
Addit. mov. (discr.)	1.75	2.421	2.016	7.37
Visual scanning	15.31	14.835	1.046	3.46
Manip. of body (clothes)	6.62	3.887	0.356	2.50
Addit. mov. (contin.)	1.04	1.791	2.167	7.61
Crying	0.10	0.647	9.272	96.89
Verbalisation	1.68	3.372	2.643	10.14

APPENDIX VIB

Observation condition 'first time alone in empty room'

Correlations

Behaviour categories		1	2	3	4	5	6	7	8	9	10	11	12
Locomotion	1												
Changes in body post./loc. patt.		+29											
Visual fixations (nr.)	2	+24	+29										
Manip. of fixtures		+14	+36	+11									
Visual fixations (dur.)		+16	+24	+11	+20								
Mov. towards one-way screen		−09	−06	−06	−12	+35							
Looking straight forw. (dur.)	3	−04	−14	−11	−17	−90	−33						
Addit. movements (discr.)		−16	−20	−15	−18	−52	−16	+44					
Visual scanning (dur.)		−27	−31	−05	−17	−82	−26	+49	+45				
Manip. of body/clothes	4	−34	−37	−03	−42	−12	+06	+06	−03	+15			
Addit. movements (contin.)		−20	−26	−15	−30	−37	−17	+27	+30	+20	+36		
Crying		−07	−07	+01	−11	+08	−11	−07	−09	−08	+20	+32	
Verbal behaviour		+14	+13	−02	−00	+06	+14	+03	+14	−10	−17	−09	−04

Behaviour patterns
1 room exploration
2 one-way screen reactions
3 passive waiting
4 body-oriented activity

APPENDIX VIIA

Observation condition 'second time in empty room'

Behaviour categories	Mean	St. deviation	Skewness	Kurtosis
Locomotion	38.90	37.459	1.451	4.76
Changes in body post/mov. patt.	13.99	11.647	3.993	29.61
Visual fixation (nr.)	15.07	5.246	0.122	3.11
Manip. of fixtures	4.99	3.466	0.660	2.95
Visual fixation (dur.)	138.93	31.752	−1.106	4.85
Mov. towards one-way-screen	2.53	3.176	1.889	7.74
Looking straight forward	25.52	25.479	1.860	9.10
Additional mov. (discr.)	1.85	2.075	1.296	4.24
Visual scanning	14.10	14.073	1.223	3.97
Manip. of body (clothes)	6.63	4.037	0.440	2.63
Additional mov. (contin.)	1.32	1.783	1.585	5.37
Crying	0.17	0.931	7.333	63.84
Verbalisation	1.63	2.802	2.403	9.50

APPENDIX VIIB

Observation condition 'second time alone in empty room'

Correlations

Behaviour categories													
Locomotion	1												
Changes in body post./loc. patt.	+39												
Visual fixations (nr.)	+44	+29											
Manip. of fixtures	+12	+14	+14										
Visual fixations (dur.)	2 +21	+03	+13	+21									
Mov. towards one-way screen	−12	−13	−17	−16	+37								
Looking straight forw. (dur.)	3 −10	−03	−17	−19	−88	+35							
Addit. movements (discr.)	−11	+03	+05	−19	−41	−13	+37						
Visual scanning (dur.)	−25	+00	−03	−18	−59	−18	+18	+27					
Manip. of body/clothes	4 −29	−13	−09	−41	−20	−10	+20	−14	+12				
Addit. movements (contin.)	−14	−15	−01	−30	−18	−14	+19	+03	+11	+59			
Crying	+39	−06	−19	−01	−06	−06	+09	−08	+00	+23	+08		
Verbal behaviour	+23	+06	+08	−01	+05	+22	−01	−01	−07	−12	−21	−03	

Behaviour patterns
1 room exploration
2 one-way screen reactions
3 passive waiting
4 body-oriented activity

Observation condition 'with blocks and passive observer'

Behaviour categories	Mean	St. deviation	Skewness	Kurtosis
Locomotion	32.50	40.661	3.218	17.25
Changes in body post./mov. patt.	37.76	25.621	0.991	4.15
Manip. of fixtures	0.66	1.914	3.235	12.65
Mov. towards one-way-screen	0.04	0.234	6.107	43.04
Glancing away from toys	2.22	7.688	8.756	91.35
Visual fixation of observer	12.22	19.697	8.530	88.50
No play activity	42.66	83.799	3.687	17.75
Manip. of body (clothes)	1.89	2.548	1.652	4.93
Crying	0.17	1.524	11.338	132.83
Additional mov. (contin.)	0.52	2.572	6.466	46.48
Additional mov. (discr.)	0.31	1.116	5.825	44.50
Tidying up	4.57	14.829	3.803	19.69
Changes in play-act. level	11.84	7.509	2.163	13.88
Play act. level I	37.63	49.452	2.184	8.89
Play act. level II	125.04	124.519	1.057	3.53
Play act. level III	318.27	154.817	−0.432	2.15
Play act. level IIE	5.20	11.879	2.674	10.23
Looking around	54.20	0.585	4.827	34.73
Looking straight forward	0.45	2.588	8.330	80.77
Verbalisation (exc. communic.)	7.37	11.874	1.915	5.92
Communication with observer	2.83	5.209	2.599	10.35
Play act. level IV	4.40	31.166	10.251	114.05

Observation condition 'with blocks and passive observer'

Behaviour categories		Correlations														
Locomotion	1															
Changes in body post./locom. patt.		+52														
Manipulation of fixtures	-	+24	+08													
Mov. towards one-way screen		+44	-09	-06												
Glancing away from toys		+58	-14	+10	+62											
Visual fix. of observer		+02	+11	-00	-01	-05										
No play activity	2	+47	-11	+37	+39	+63	-00									
Manip. body/clothes (dur.)	3	+02	-25	+04	+19	+27	-06	+42								
Crying		-05	-12	+03	-02	-02	-05	+36	+27							
Addit. movements (contin.)		-07	-14	-05	+01	+03	+01	+32	+46	+44						
Addit. movements (discr.)	-	+05	-11	-06	-00	+10	-08	+04	+10	-02	+03					
Tidying up		-00	-01	+02	+07	+08	-04	+07	-04	-01	-02	+40				
Changes in play act. level	4	-14	+10	+05	-02	-15	+09	-07	+05	-13	-03	-01	+03			
Play activity level I		+11	+25	+07	-01	-10	+01	-03	-14	-07	-09	-09	+15	+33		
Play activity level II		+06	+26	+10	-15	-09	+06	-21	-20	-10	-04	-07	-03	+13	+19	
Play activity level III	5	-33	-19	-29	-11	-24	-03	-08	-01	-18	-12	+05	-16	-18	-47	-72

Behaviour patterns
1 gross body activity
2 no play activity
3 body-oriented activity ('distressed')
4 low level play
5 high level play

115

APPENDIX IXA

Observation condition 'alone with a variety of toys'

Behaviour categories	Mean	St. deviation	Skewness	Kurtosis
Locomotion	35.43	21.089	1.644	8.47
Changes in body post/mov. patt.	46.86	23.228	1.726	9.48
Manip. of fixtures (dur.)	0.48	1.500	6.791	61.39
Mov. towards one-way-screen	0.11	0.499	4.784	25.77
Looking straight forward	0.40	1.630	5.280	32.06
Manip. of body (clothes)	1.81	3.274	2.822	12.15
Crying	1.75	8.152	6.994	60.98
Verbalisation	11.71	15.054	1.793	6.95
Addit. mov. (contin.)	0.99	6.070	9.290	97.00
Addit. mov. (discr.)	0.47	1.653	5.784	40.10
Glancing away from toys	3.77	3.817	1.657	5.86
Changes of play activity	30.12	16.075	4.464	34.51
Changes in play act. level	21.66	9.895	−0.098	2.96
Play act. level I	39.43	49.145	3.830	28.16
Play act. level II	212.91	161.416	0.846	5.46
Play act. level IIE	38.63	37.457	1.412	5.32
Play act. level III	384.70	180.782	0.348	2.71
Longest play activity	149.55	87.897	1.583	7.32
No play activity	56.09	113.472	3.275	13.75
Play act. level IV	39.48	79.405	2.838	12.71
Tidying up	7.47	21.670	3.375	14.27
Looking around	2.63	2.333	1.326	5.82

116

APPENDIX IXB

Observation condition 'alone with a variety of toys'

Behaviour categories		Correlations
Locomotion	1	
Body post./locom. patt.		+78
Manip. of fixt. (dur.)	-	+02 −03
Mov. towards one-way screen		+09 −03 +21
Looking straight forw.		+04 +11 +39 +24
Manip. of body (clothes)		+03 +11 +21 +52 +37
Crying		+09 −12 +37 +10 +37 +26
Verbalization	2	+06 +05 +06 −04 −09 +02 +04
Addit. movem. (cont.)		+03 +07 +16 +12 +19 +35 +12 +23
Addit. movem. (discr.)		+92 +03 +26 +00 +01 +05 +01 +29 +56
Glancing away from toys	-	+20 +04 +07 +06 +06 +17 +03 +33 +01 +11
Changes of play act.	3	+24 +23 −11 −02 −11 +06 +01 +12 +08 −01 +36
Changes in play act. level		+31 +22 −00 +14 +06 +19 +05 +06 +08 +04 +30 +32
Play act. level I		+19 +03 +12 +13 +15 +15 +06 +12 +21 +16 +40 +21 +32
Play act. level II	4	+15 +15 −13 +03 −18 −09 −10 +06 −14 +02 +05 +37 +17 +01
Play act. level IIE		+06 +13 −11 −05 −11 −14 −03 −11 −12 −02 −03 +19 +14 +08 +29
Play act. level III	5	−19 −09 −17 −19 −18 −16 −11 +03 −18 −14 −22 +32 −25 +38 −54 −23
Longest play activity		−24 −19 −11 −17 −09 −10 −12 −03 −08 −11 −13 −18 −35 −16 −26 −17 +46
No play activity (dur.)	6	+08 +02 +57 +36 +56 +58 +37 +07 +52 +28 +15 −14 +01 +23 −31 −18 −16 −10

Behaviour patterns
1 gross body activity
2 non-specific activity
3 low level play
4 exploratory play
5 high level play
6 no play activity

117

APPENDIX XA

Observation condition 'alone with one non-motivating toy'

Behaviour categories	Mean	St. deviation	Skewness	Kurtosis
Locomotion	10.40	17.376	3.290	15.86
Changes in body post./mov. patt.	10.47	8.091	0.730	3.12
Manip. of fixtures	1.20	2.537	3.193	16.41
Mov. towards one-way-screen	0.44	1.266	3.486	15.95
Glancing away from toys	1.64	3.023	2.813	11.83
No play activity	59.63	80.783	1.398	3.80
Looking around	0.78	1.418	2.469	9.32
Looking straight forward	0.53	1.545	4.301	23.60
Manip. of body (clothes)	2.39	3.911	2.090	6.99
Additional mov. (contin.)	0.96	2.774	3.373	14.27
Changes in play act. level	1.47	2.306	1.797	5.89
Changes of play act.	7.42	4.824	0.252	2.42
Play act. level I	40.53	50.294	1.813	6.52
Play act. level III	68.27	83.379	1.115	3.27
Longest play act.	75.88	61.028	1.213	4.97
Play act. level II	80.86	73.133	0.916	3.24
Play act. level IIE	2.59	7.616	3.194	12.92
Additional mov. (discr.)	0.63	1.439	3.412	15.93
Tidying up	17.39	34.975	2.489	9.50
Verbalisation	3.32	5.249	1.962	6.29
Crying	0.35	1.834	7.310	63.75

Observation condition 'alone with one non-motivating toy'

Correlations

Behaviour categories		1	2	3	4	5	6	7	8	9	10	11	12	13	14	15
Locomotion	1															
Body posture/locom. patt.		+59														
Manip. of fixtures (dur.)		+64	+40													
Mov. towards one-way screen		+20	+25	+34												
Glancing away from toys	-	+28	+17	+33	+36											
No play activity (dur.)	2	+49	+32	+74	+31	+37										
Looking around	3	+09	+19	+33	-01	+25	+47									
Looking straight ahead		+15	-24	+32	-04	+28	+59	+59								
Manip. of body/clothes (dur.)		+29	+18	+56	+22	+30	+76	+48	+67							
Addit. movements (contin.)		+16	+05	+25	+06	+25	+44	+34	+38	+46						
Changes in play act. level	4	+06	+27	-06	+10	+13	-12	-07	-17	-11	-09					
Changes of play act.		-04	+27	-10	+05	-08	-20	-02	-14	-17	-07	+23				
Play act. level I		+16	+25	-05	+06	+08	-16	+08	-12	-12	-01	+31	+46			
Play act. level II	-	-10	-12	-25	-06	-14	-34	-18	-21	+27	+18	+16	+34	+09		
Play act. level III	5	-30	-21	-31	-14	-15	-37	-24	-22	-23	-16	+12	-01	-26	-21	
Longest play activity		-16	-03	-33	-15	-11	-43	-24	-29	-19	+01	+15	+01	+15	-33	+40

Behaviour patterns
1 room-oriented behaviour
2 no play activity
3 passive waiting (body-oriented act.)
4 low level play
5 high level play

APPENDIX XI

Correlations* among the behaviour patterns in the six observation conditions (N = 117)

Behaviour patterns	Observ. cond.	Correlations* among the behaviour patterns in the six observation conditions (N = 117)
Room explorat.	Alone 1	
Room explorat.	Alone 2	+35
Room explorat.	Mother	+29 +23
One-way screen	Alone 1	+12 −03 +07
One-way screen	Alone 2	−08 −02 +09 +29
One-way screen	Mother	+21 +11 +54 +18 +16
Verbal contact	Mother	−03 +12 +04 +13 −09 +04
Visual contact	Mother	−02 +08 +22 −06 −19 −01
Gross body act.	Blocks	+11 +19 +30 +02 +11 +12 +10 +17
Gross body act.	Vartoys	+26 +26 +37 −05 −02 +15 +10 +08 +44
Low level play	Blocks	+06 +04 +17 −06 +10 +09 +07 +15 +20 +17
Low level play	Vartoys	−09 +03 +05 −19 −03 +05 −07 −02 +17 +22 +10
Exploratory play	Vartoys	+17 +19 +22 −14 −05 +17 +01 +11 +12 +37 +23 +27
Low level play	Onetoy	+11 +06 +06 +02 +13 +07 −04 −07 +04 +07 +25 +12 +19
Room orient. act.	Onetoy	+23 +08 +24 +01 −01 +16 +15 +08 +12 +23 +17 +09 +11 +11
Passive waiting	Onetoy	−01 −08 −02 −00 −05 −06 −10 +07 +07 +01 +11 +15 +08 −17 +31
No play act.	Blocks	−13 −01 −00 −08 −02 −16 +10 +09 +23 +10 −09 +25 −24 −05 +02 +11
No play act.	Vartoys	−28 −32 −17 +13 −08 −17 +01 −05 −10 −06 −10 −26 −31 −28 −06 +24 +33
No play act.	Onetoy	+06 −04 +06 +01 −03 +03 +12 +13 +12 +14 +12 −05 −25 +62 +73 +14 +30
Tidying up**	Blocks	+03 −22 −08 +10 −10 +05 +02 −18 −05 +08 −03 +17 −13 −07 −02 +10 +06 +25 +10
Body-orient. act.	Alone 1	−48 −29 −13 −23 −02 −08 −18 −04 −16 −21 −11 +08 −24 −04 −16 +12 +06 +23 +05 +02
Body-orient. act.	Alone 2	−26 −29 −19 +02 −20 −07 −11 −16 −13 −19 −11 −35 −09 −01 −17 +21 +34 +15 +15 +30
Body-orient. act.	Blocks	−18 −20 −05 +17 +14 −10 +05 −18 −12 −13 −09 +09 −25 +02 −07 +16 +43 +39 +12 +07 +16 +24
Non-specif. act.	Vartoys	−16 −16 −03 +25 +19 −03 +08 +02 −06 +05 +06 +27 −12 −06 +07 +23 +38 +12 +34 −01 −02 +23
Passive waiting	Mother	−13 −13 −47 −08 −01 −48 −19 −30 −10 −17 −11 +01 −14 −12 −13 +08 +06 +11 −01 +07 +16 +23 +14 −07
Passive waiting	Alone 1	−32 −08 −15 −78 −16 −11 −07 −07 −01 −01 +16 +17 −04 +04 +09 +06 −12 −04 −01 +30 −00 −13 −13 +15
Passive waiting	Alone 2	+03 −19 −17 −11 −73 −15 −02 −01 −16 −01 −13 −05 +13 +01 −05 +13 +01 −05 −04 +08 −03 +16 −17 −03 +02 +19
Close contact	Mother	−19 −22 −45 −06 −13 −31 −13 −25 −18 −08 −19 −08 −10 −01 −10 +10 +07 +23 +4 +16 +14 +21 +24 +05 +36 +20 +16
High level play	Blocks	−01 −01 −13 +17 −03 −07 −03 −13 −35 −22 −75 −26 −12 −12 −12 +31 +00 −11 −01 +09 −02 −05 −10 +02 −04 +15 +17
High level play	Vartoys	−06 −09 −17 −06 +06 −09 −04 −08 −01 −21 −18 −36 −49 +10 −17 −21 −05 −19 −27 −03 +16 −03 −14 +08 −03 −01 +02 +19
High level play	Onetoy	−01 −09 −06 +06 −07 −05 −10 −03 −18 −05 −17 −14 −02 −10 −10 −37 −23 −19 +73 −07 +08 −16 −06 +01 −08 −03 −01 +14 +25
School train. parents***		−11 −08 −08 +08 −04 +03 +08 −14 −10 −06 −14 −00 −13 −18 +06 −06 −09 +05 +17 +03 +10 +03 +06 −02 −01 +05 +12 −04 +08
IQ child (Stanf. Binet)		−00 −13 −00 +09 +14 −05 +07 +01 −23 −16 −15 −27 −18 −10 −12 −17 −08 −10 +03 −10 +01 +10 +08 +15 −10 −05 −09 −17 +04 +20 +17 +16 +34

*Coefficient of .18 significant below 5%, of .23 below 1% level (two-tailed)

**"Tidying up" is excluded from the overall-analysis, because of too low frequency of occurrence

***Combination of maternal and paternal levels of school training

Components of neurobehavioural profiles: differences between means*

With mother in the novel empty room

		Boys				Girls	
		means		*t-values*		*means*	*t-values*
variables	N	39	22	39-22	26	30	26-30
Sensorimotor		8.3	9.3	1.79	8.9	10.3	3.34
Maturation of functions		5.4	5.7	0.69	6.4	8.2	3.54
Maturation of responses		2.4	2.8	1.22	2.5	3.2	2.62
Choreiform movements		1.2	1.1	0.35	1.6	1.5	0.31
Co-ordination		3.8	4.2	1.24	4.0	4.6	2.47
Posture		4.2	4.7	1.86	4.5	4.2	0.68
Verbal contact		503.3	496.6	2.58	499.2	499.9	0.26
Visual contact		501.1	496.6	1.84	503.1	501.1	0.71
Close contact		493.2	511.9	4.73	491.6	505.3	3.28
Passive wait./body or. act.		487.6	514.8	4.52	486.3	512.9	4.45
Reactions one-way screen		508.8	491.1	4.98	505.1	491.5	3.71
Room exploration		521.6	477.3	7.64	512.5	485.8	4.22

First time alone in the empty room

		Boys				Girls	
		means		*t-values*		*means*	*t-values*
variables	N	28	33	28-33	20	36	20-36
Sensorimotor		7.6	9.5	4.10	8.7	10.2	3.41
Maturation of functions		5.2	5.7	0.94	5.6	8.3	5.48
Maturation of responses		2.0	2.9	3.26	2.2	3.5	4.34
Choreiform movements		0.8	1.5	2.54	1.6	1.5	0.31
Co-ordination		3.5	4.3	2.71	3.6	4.7	4.69
Posture		3.8	4.8	4.51	4.5	4.3	0.65
Passive waiting		490.0	510.8	3.81	518.3	487.9	4.93
Body-oriented activity		489.9	503.8	3.55	510.6	500.5	2.38
Reactions one-way screen		505.6	493.2	3.82	486.4	510.2	5.47
Room exploration		516.7	489.1	4.61	495.0	494.4	0.09

*As a rough estimation of the significance of the differences between means, t-values are preferred to p-values, because these are not random samples from two populations. One might consider t-values above 2 to be relevant.

Scores in the behaviour patterns (variable 7 and lower in each table) were obtained by summation of standard scores in the separate categories and adding 500 to the sum in order to avoid negative values.

Second time alone in the empty room

variables	N	Boys means 15	Boys means 46	t-value 15-46	Girls means 19	Girls means 37	t-value 19-37
Sensorimotor		9.2	6.9	4.09	8.4	10.3	4.60
Matur. of functions		5.7	4.9	1.63	6.0	8.0	3.97
Matur. of responses		2.9	1.3	5.12	2.0	3.3	5.39
Choreiform mov.		1.2	1.1	0.31	1.4	1.7	0.89
Co-ordination		4.0	3.7	0.86	3.6	4.7	5.16
Posture		4.8	3.2	6.23	4.5	4.3	0.64
Passive waiting		493.8	525.9	6.08	513.6	492.3	3.92
Body-orient, act.		495.4	497.3	0.40	511.7	502.9	1.65
React. one-way scr.		505.9	483.2	5.32	488.5	506.7	4.29
Room exploration		506.5	486.3	2.54	493.7	497.8	0.59

With blocks and a passive observer

variables	N	Boys means 36	Boys means 25	t-value 36-25	Girls means 20	Girls means 8	Girls means 28	t-values 20-8	t-values 20-28	t-values 8-28
Sensorimotor		8.2	9.3	2.02	8.3	10.6	10.4	3.00	4.94	0.71
Matur. of functions		5.2	5.9	1.65	6.0	7.8	8.2	2.33	4.13	0.51
Matur. of responses		2.3	2.9	1.89	2.2	3.5	3.2	3.02	3.65	0.93
Choreiform mov.		0.7	1.8	4.28	1.5	1.8	1.5	0.58	0.00	0.61
Co-ordination		3.8	4.1	0.94	3.5	4.9	4.8	4.20	6.78	0.62
Posture		4.2	4.7	1.92	4.4	4.9	4.2	1.50	0.59	1.49
High level play		494.1	509.6	7.42	500.2	497.0	503.5	0.89	1.56	2.42
Low level play		514.6	483.2	6.52	504.3	489.6	497.3	2.06	1.49	1.44
No play activity		499.8	496.8	2.12	497.8	514.9	497.2	3.40	0.67	4.27
Body-orient. act.		496.5	496.1	0.17	499.9	536.8	495.2	3.30	1.61	4.53
Gross body act.		507.7	496.1	2.51	493.3	511.4	495.8	2.49	0.75	2.40

With a variety of toys

variables	N	Boys means 25	Boys means 36	t-value 25-36	Girls means 26	Girls means 30	t-value 26-30
Sensorimotor		7.3	9.6	4.99	8.6	10.6	5.37
Matur. of functions		5.1	5.8	1.64	6.2	8.3	4.20
Matur. of responses		1.8	3.1	4.62	2.5	3.2	2.62
Choreiform mov.		0.9	1.3	1.42	1.7	1.4	0.92
Co-ordination		3.4	4.3	3.05	4.0	4.6	2.58
Posture		3.8	4.8	4.20	3.9	4.8	3.51
High level play		499.3	492.8	2.57	500.8	516.2	3.07
Explorative play		508.7	506.0	0.50	501.0	480.2	4.52
Low level play		489.8	506.5	4.17	502.9	488.3	3.07
No play activity		496.2	501.8	2.50	498.9	503.0	1.19
Non specific act.		492.3	501.4	2.90	499.9	503.8	0.43
Gross body act.		498.6	507.8	2.13	495.5	491.1	1.31

With one non-motivating toy (boys)

variables	N	means				t-values					
		17	22	12	10	17-22	17-12	17-10	22-12	22-10	12-10
Sensorimotor		6.8	9.5	8.5	10.2	4.55	2.24	4.49	1.77	1.30	2.65
Matur. of functions		4.7	5.0	6.2	7.1	0.71	2.61	4.87	2.10	4.02	1.27
Matur. of responses		1.4	3.0	3.0	3.0	4.50	4.00	3.65	0.00	0.00	0.00
Choreiform mov.		0.9	0.6	1.8	2.1	1.16	2.02	3.33	3.51	6.23	0.61
Co-ordination		3.1	4.3	4.1	4.5	3.38	2.01	2.94	0.58	0.68	0.93
Posture		3.3	4.8	4.8	4.9	5.12	3.71	3.80	0.00	0.70	0.48
High level play		497.8	496.9	484.6	519.7	0.29	4.20	3.08	4.40	3.66	4.53
Low level play		507.9	514.0	487.5	482.2	0.96	2.80	3.78	3.78	4.70	0.77
No play activity		497.9	497.1	519.8	495.0	0.48	0.65	1.45	1.68	1.09	0.86
Passive waiting		492.9	492.1	552.2	489.3	0.16	5.05	0.71	5.46	0.45	4.17
Room oriented act.		499.7	502.6	556.3	481.4	0.37	3.72	2.03	4.04	2.72	4.17

With one non-motivating toy (girls)

variables	N	means						t-values*		
		15	5	4	4	19	9	15-9	15-19	19-9
Sensorimotor		8.3	9.2	9.3	10.5	10.5	10.4	4.12	2.76	0.35
Matur. of functions		6.1	5.4	7.0	8.8	8.2	8.3	3.38	2.92	0.12
Mat. of responses		2.1	1.6	3.8	3.8	3.3	3.3	4.34	3.72	0.00
Choreiform mov.		1.5	2.0	1.0	0.3	1.5	2.3	0.00	1.72	1.69
Coordination		3.5	4.8	4.5	4.3	4.6	4.8	3.72	3.39	0.90
Posture		4.6	3.6	1.5	5.0	4.8	4.6	1.05	0.00	0.97
High level play		502.5	492.4	508.8	497.5	515.8	486.3	2.35	2.53	5.83
Low level play		492.7	526.8	509.0	521.0	499.7	490.0	1.47	0.44	1.91
No play activity		496.3	498.0	495.3	497.8	494.8	516.2	0.87	6.96	1.12
Passive waiting		489.2	511.2	490.5	495.8	485.6	545.9	1.54	4.18	5.08
Room-oriented act.		486.7	490.8	492.0	528.5	482.7	519.0	0.55	2.36	3.60

*Groups comprising five or less cases were not included.

REFERENCES

Abrams, A. L. (1968) 'Delayed and irregular maturation versus minimal brain injury.' *Clinical Pediatrics,* **7,** 344.

Arsenian, J. M. (1943) 'Young children in an insecure situation.' *Journal of Abnormal and Social Psychology,* **38,** 225.

Barendrecht, J. T. (1969) 'An attempt at destruction of a proportionality.' Paper submitted to the XIX International Congress of Psychology, London.

Bax, M., Mac Keith, R. (1963) *Minimal Cerebral Dysfunction.* Little Club Clinics in Developmental Medicine, no. 10. London: S.I.M.P./Heinemann.

Bax, M. (1972) 'The active and the over-active school child.' *Developmental Medicine and Child Neurology,* **14,** 83.

Beintema, D. J. (1968) *A Neurological Study of Newborn Infants.* Clinics in Developmental Medicine, no. 28. London: S.I.M.P./Heinemann.

Bell, R. Q. (1964) 'Structuring parent-child interaction situations for direct observation.' *Child Development,* **35,** 1009.

—— (1968) 'Adaptation of small wrist watches for mechanical recording of activity in infants and children.' *Journal of Experimental Child Psychology,* **6,** 302.

—— Weller, G. M., Waldrop, M. F. (1971) 'Newborn and preschooler: organization of behavior and relations between periods.' *Monographs of the Society for Research in Child Development,* **36,** nos. 1, 2.

Benton, A. L. (1962) 'Behavioural indices of brain injury in school children.' *Child Development,* **33,** 199.

—— (1973) 'Minimal brain dysfunction from a neuropsychological point of view.' *Annals of the New York Academy of Sciences,* **205,**

Berkson, G. (1969) 'Stereotyped movements of mental defectives. V. Ward behavior and its relation to an experimental task.' *American Journal of Mental Deficiency,* **69,** 253.

Berlyne, D. E. (1960) *Conflict, Arousal and Curiosity.* New York: McGraw-Hill.

Birch, H. G. (1964) *Brain Damage in Children.* Baltimore: Williams and Wilkins.

—— Demb, H. (1953) 'The formation and extinction of conditional reflexes in "brain-damaged" and mongoloid children.' *Journal of Nervous and Mental Disease,* **129,** 162.

Blau, A. (1936) 'Mental changes following head trauma in children.' *Archives of Neurology and Psychiatry,* **35,** 723.

Bond, E. D. (1932) 'Postencephalitic, ordinary and extraordinary children.' *Journal of Pediatrics,* **1,** 310.

Boring, E. G. (1960) 'Lashley and cortical integration.' *In* Beach, F. A., Hebb, D. O., Morgan, C. G., Nissen, H. W. (Eds.) *The Neurophysiology of Lashley.* New York: McGraw-Hill.

Bowlby, J. (1971) *Attachment. Attachment and Loss Series, vol. I.* Harmondsworth: Penguin.

Bowden, D. M., Goldman, P. S., Rosvold, H. E. (1971) 'Free behavior of rhesus monkeys following lesions of the dorso-lateral and orbital prefrontal cortex in infancy.' *Experimental Brain Research,* **12,** 265.

Connolly, K., Stratton, P. (1968) 'Developmental changes in associated movements.' *Developmental Medicine and Child Neurology,* **10,** 49.

Costello, A. J. (1973) 'The reliability of direct observation.' *Bulletin of the British Psychological Society,* **26,** 105.

Cranach, M. von (1969) 'The role of orienting behavior in human interaction.' *In* Esser, A. H. (Ed.) *The Use of Space by Animals and Men.* Bloomington: Indiana University Press.

Crinella, F. M. (1973) 'Identification of brain dysfunction syndromes in children through profile analysis.' *Journal of Abnormal and Social Psychology,* **82,** 33.

Cromwell, R. L., Baumeister, A., Hawkins, W. F. (1963) 'Research in activity level.' *In* Ellis, N. R. (Ed.) *Handbook of Mental Deficiency: Psychological Theory and Research.* New York: McGraw-Hill.

Darwin, C. (1877) 'A biographical sketch of an infant.' *Mind,* **2,** 285.

Dijkstra, J. (1960) *De Prognostische Betekenis van Neurologische Afwijkingen bij Pasgeboren Kinderen.* Groningen: Thesis.

Dinnage, R. (1970) 'The handicapped child.' *Studies in Child Development: Research Review vol. I.* London: Longman.

Eisenberg, L. (1957) 'Psychiatric implications of brain damage in children.' *Psychiatric Quarterly,* **31,** 72.

Ellgrin, J. H. (1969) *Die Beurteilung des Blickes auf Punkte innerhalb des Gesichts.* New York: McGraw-Hill.

Fraser, M. S., Wilks, J. (1959) 'The residual effects of neonatal asphyxia.' *Journal of Obstetrics and Gynaecology of the British Empire,* **66,** 748.

Gershaw, N. J., Schwarz, J. C. (1971) 'The effects of a familiar toy and mother's presence on exploratory and attachment behaviors in young children.' *Child Development,* **42,** 1662.

130

Gibson, W. A. (1959) 'Three multivariate models: factor analysis, latent structure analysis and latent profile analysis.' *Psychometrica,* **24,** 229.
—— (1962) 'Class assignment in the latent profile model.' *Journal of Applied Psychology,* **46,** 399.
Goldfried, M. R., Kent, R. N. (1972) 'Traditional versus behavioural personality assessment: a comparison of methodological and theoretical assumptions.' *Psychological Bulletin,* **77,** 409.
Gomez, M. R. (1967) 'Minimal cerebral dysfunction (maximal neurological confusion).' *Clinical Pediatrics,* **6,** 589.
Gottfried, A. W. (1973) 'Intellectual consequences of perinatal anoxia.' *Psychological Bulletin,* **80,** 232.
Grant, W. W., Boelsche, A. N., Zin, D. (1973) 'Developmental patterns of two motor functions.' *Developmental Medicine and Child Neurology,* **15,** 171.
Groot, A. D. de (1961) *Methodologie.* The Hague: Mouton,
Hall, G. S. (1891) 'The contents of children's minds on entering school.' *Pedagogical Seminary,* **1,** 139.
Hinde, R. A. (1966) *Animal Behavior: A Synthesis of Ethology and Comparative Psychology.* New York: McGraw-Hill.
—— (1971) 'Some problems in the study of development.' *In* Tobach, E., Aronson, L. R., Shaw, E. (Eds.) *The Biopsychology of Development.* New York: Academic Press.
Hohman, L. B. (1922) 'Post-encephalitic behavior disorders.' *Johns Hopkins Hospital Bulletin,* **33,** 372.
Hooff, J. A. R. A. M. van (1971) *Aspects of the Social Behaviour and Communication in Human and Higher Non-human Primates.* Rotterdam: Bronder-Offset.
Huessy, H. R. (1967) 'Study of the prevalence and therapy of the choreatiform syndrome or hyperkinesis in rural Vermont.' *Acta Paedopsychiatrica,* **34,** 130.
Hughes, J. (1971) 'Electroencephalography and learning disabilities.' *In* Myklebust, H. R. (Ed.) *Progress in Learning Disabilities,* vol. 2. New York: Grune and Stratton.
Hutt, C. (1966) 'Exploration and play in children.' *Symposia of the Zoological Society of London,* **18,** 61.
—— (1967) 'Effects of stimulus novelty on manipulatory exploration in an infant.' *Journal of Child Psychology and Psychiatry,* **8,** 241.
—— (1968) 'Exploration of novelty in children with and without upper C.N.S. lesions and some effects of auditory and visual incentives.' *Acta Psychologica,* **28,** 150.
—— (1970) 'Curiosity in young children.' *Science Journal,* **6,** 68.
—— Hutt, S. J., Ounsted, C. A. (1963) 'A method for the study of children's behaviour.' *Developmental Medicine and Child Neurology,* **5,** 233.
—— —— —— (1965) 'The behaviour of children with and without upper C.N.S. lesions.' *Behaviour,* **24,** 246.
—— —— —— (1964) 'Hyperactivity in a group of epileptic (and some non-epileptic) brain-damaged children. A behavioural study with some implications for education.' *Epilepsia,* **5,** 334.
—— —— (1970) *Direct Observation and Measurement of Behavior.* Springfield, Ill.: C. C. Thomas.
Ingram, T. T. S. (1973) 'Soft signs.' *Developmental Medicine and Child Neurology,* **15,** 527.
Jaspars, J. M. F., Oever, A. C. C. van de, Theunissen, H. L. A. (1963) 'Het observeren van ogencontact.' *Nederlands Tijdschrift voor de Psychologie en haar Grensgebieden,* **28,** 67.
Johnson, D. A. (1972) 'Developmental aspects of recovery of function following septal lesions in the infant rat.' *Journal of Comparative and Physiological Psychology,* **78,** 331.
Kalverboer, A. F. (1971*a*) 'Observations of exploratory behaviour of pre-school children, alone and in the presence of the mother.' *Psychiatria, Neurologia, Neurochirurgia,* **74,** 43.
—— (1971*b*) 'Observations of free-field behaviour in preschool boys and girls in relation to neurological findings.' *In* Stoelinga, G. B., van der Werff ten Bosch, J. J. (Eds.) *Normal and Abnormal Development of Brain and Behaviour.* Leyden: University Press.
—— (1971*c*) 'Over de relatie tussen neurologische dysfuncties en gedrag bij kinderen.' *In* de Wit, J., Bolle, H., Jessurun Cardozo-van Hoorn (Eds.). *Psychologen over het Kind.* Groningen: Wolters-Noordhoff.
—— Touwen, B. C. L., Prechtl, H. F. R. (1973) 'Follow-up of infants at risk of minor brain dysfunction.' *Annals of the New York Academy of Sciences,* **205,** 172.
Kimble, D. P., Rogers, L., Hendrickson, C. W. (1967) 'Hippocampal lesions disrupt maternal, not sexual, behavior in the albino rat.' *Journal of Comparative and Physiological Psychology,* **63,** 401.
Kinsbourne, M. (1973) 'Minimal brain dysfunction as a neurodevelopmental lag.' *Annals of the New York Academy of Science,* **205.**
Klein, M. (1960) *The Psychoanalysis of Children.* New York: Grove Press.
Knobloch, H., Pasamanick, B. (1963) 'Predicting intellectual potential in infancy.' *American Journal of Diseases of Children,* **106,** 43.
—— —— (1966) 'Prospective studies on the epidemiology of reproductive casualty: methods, findings and some implications.' *Merrill-Palmer Quarterly,* **12,** 27.

131

—— Rider, R., Harper, P., Pasamanick, B. (1956) 'Neuropsychiatric sequelae of prematurity.' *Journal of the American Medical Association,* **161,** 581.

Lashley, K. S. (1930) 'Basic neural mechanisms in behavior.' *Psychological Review,* **37,** 1.

—— (1950) 'In search of the engram.' *Symposia of the Society for Experimental Biology,* **4,** 454.

—— (1951) 'The problem of serial order in behavior.' *In* Jeffress, L. A. (Ed.) *Cerebral Mechanisms in Behavior: The Hixon Symposium.* New York: Wiley.

—— (1958) 'Cerebral organization and behavior.' *In The Brain and Human Behavior. Proceedings of the Association for Research in Nervous and Mental Disease,* **36,** 1.

Lazarsfeld, P. F. (1950) 'The logical and mathematical foundation of latent structure analysis.' *In* Stouffer, S. A. (Ed.) *Measurement and Prediction.* Princeton: Princeton University Press.

—— Henry, N. W. (1968) *Latent Structure Analysis.* New York: Houghton, Mifflin.

Lowenfeld, M. (1935) *Play in Childhood.* London: Gollancz.

Luria, A. R. (1973) *The Working Brain.* Harmondsworth: Penguin Books.

Lurie, L. A., Levy, S. (1942) 'Personality changes and behavior disorders of children following pertussis. A report based on the study of five hundred problem children.' *Journal of the American Medical Association,* **120,** 890.

Mardberg, B. (1971) 'A preliminary computer program for the solution of LPA due to Green's method.' Stockholm. Swedish Council for Personnel Administration.

—— (1974) LPA2 (A clustering program). Program description. Internal Research Report from the Psychological Institute of Bergen, Norway, **5,** no. 2.

McGrew, W. C. (1972) *An Ethological Study of Children's Behavior.* New York: Academic Press.

Mellins, R. B., Jenkins, C. D. (1955) 'Epidemiological and psychological study of lead poisoning in children.' *Journal of the American Medical Association,* **158,** 15.

Murphy, H. M., Brown, T. B. (1970) 'Effects of hippocampal lesions on simple and preferential consummatory behavior in the rat.' *Journal of Comparative and Physiological Psychology,* **72,** 404.

Musty, E. (1969) 'On hippocampal lesions on simple and preferential consummatory behaviour in the rat.' *Journal of Comparative Physiology and Psychology,* **72,** 404.

Myklebust, H. R. (1973) 'Identification and diagnosis of children with learning disabilities: an interdisciplinary study of criteria.' *Seminars in Psychiatry,* **5,** 55.

Nooteboom, W. E. (1967) *Some Psychological Aspects of the Choreatiform Syndrome. Development of Intelligence.* Assen: Van Gorcum.

Nunnally, J. C. (1967) *Psychometric Theory.* New York: McGraw-Hill.

Ounsted, C. A. (1955) 'The hyperkinetic syndrome in epileptic children.' *Lancet,* **ii,** 303.

Paine, R. (1968) 'Syndromes of "minimal cerebral damage".' *Pediatric Clinics of North America,* **15,** 779.

Peacock, L. J., Williams, M. (1962) 'An ultrasonic device for recording activity.' *American Journal of Psychology,* **75,** 648.

Pestalozzi, J. (1774) 'A father's diary.' *In* Guimps, R. de (Ed.) (1904) *Pestalozzi, His Life and Work.* New York: Appleton.

Piaget, J. (1971) *Biology and Knowledge.* Chicago: University of Chicago Press.

Prechtl, H. F. R. (1965) 'Prognostic value of neurological signs in the newborn infant.' *Proceedings of the Royal Society of Medicine,* **58,** 3.

—— (1968) 'Neurological findings in newborn infants after pre- and paranatal complications.' *In* Jonxis, J. H. P., Visser, H. K. A., Troelstra, J. A. (Eds.) *Aspects of Prematurity and Dysmaturity.* Leiden: Stenfert Kroese.

—— (1972) 'Strategy and validity of early detection of neurological dysfunction.' *In* Douglas, C. P., Holt, K. S. (Eds.) *Mental Retardation, Prenatal Diagnosis and Infant Assessment.* London: Butterworth.

—— (1973) 'Das leicht hirngeschädigte Kind. Theoretische Überlegungen zu einem praktischen Problem.' *In* Rümke, C., Boeke, P. E., Dijk, W. K. van: *Van Kinderanalyse tot Y-Chromosoom.* Deventer: Van Loghum Staterus.

—— Beintema, D. J. (1964) *The Neurological Examination of the Full-term Newborn Infant.* Clinics in Developmental Medicine, no. 12. London: S.I.M.P./Heinemann.

—— Stemmer, C. (1962) 'The choreiform syndrome in children.' *Developmental Medicine and Child Neurology,* **4,** 119.

Preyer, W. (1882) *Die Seele des Kindes.* Leipzig: T. Grieben.

Rheingold, H. L. (1969) 'The effects of a strange environment on the behavior of infants.' *Determinants of Infant Behavior.* **4,** 137.

Richardson, S. A., Birch, H. G., Hertzig, M. E. (1973) 'School performance of children who were severely malnourished in infancy.' *American Journal of Mental Deficiency,* **77,** 623.

Rosenfeld, G. B., Bradley, C. (1948) 'Childhood behavior sequelae of asphyxia in infancy with special reference to pertussis and asphyxia neonatorum.' *Pediatrics,* **2,** 74.

Rosner, B. S. (1970) 'Brain functions.' *Annual Review of Psychology,* **21,** 555.

Routh, D. K., Roberts, R. D. (1972) 'Minimal brain dysfunction in children: failure to find evidence for a behavioral syndrome.' *Psychological Reports,* **31,** 307.

Rutter, M., Graham, P., Birch, H. G. (1966) 'Interrelations between the choreiform syndrome, reading disability and psychiatric disorder in children of 8-11.' *Developmental Medicine and Child Neurology,* **8,** 149.

—— —— Yule, W. (1970) *A Neuropsychiatric Study in Childhood.* Clinics in Developmental Medicine, no. 35/36. London: S.I.M.P./Heinemann.

Sainz, A. (1966) 'Hyperkinetic disease of children: diagnosis and therapy.' *Diseases of the Nervous System,* **27,** 48.

Satterfield, J. H., Dawson, M. E. (1971) 'Electrodermal correlates of hyperactivity in children.' *Psychophysiology,* **8,** 191.

Schachter, F. F., Apgar, V. (1959) 'Perinatal asphyxia and psychological signs of brain damage in childhood.' *Pediatrics,* **24,** 1016.

Schaefer, E. S., Droppleman, L. E., Kalverboer, A. F. (1965) 'Development of a classroom behavior checklist and factor analyses of children's school behavior in the United States and the Netherlands.' Proceedings of the Conference of the Society for Research in Child Development, San Francisco.

Schain, R. J. (1970) 'Neurological evaluation of children with learning disorders.' *Neuropädiatrie,* **1,** 307.

Schulman, J. L., Kaspar, J. C., Throne, F. M. (1965) *Brain Damage and Behavior; a Clinical-Experimental Study.* Springfield, Ill.: C. C. Thomas.

Schwartz, S. (1964) 'Effect of neonatal cortical lesions and early environmental factors on adult rat behavior.' *Journal of Comparative and Physiological Psychology,* **57,** 72.

Slotnik, B. M. (1967) 'Disturbances of maternal behavior in the rat following lesions of the cingulate cortex.' *Behaviour,* **29,** 204.

Sperry, R. W. (1968) 'Plasticity of neural maturation.' *Developmental Biology,* suppl. 2, 306.

Standing, E. M. (1957) *Maria Montessori, Her Life and Her Work.* London: Hollis, Carter.

Stemmer, C. J. (1964) *Choreatiforme Bewegingsonrust.* Groningen: Van Denderen.

Stewart, M. A., Pitts, F. N., Craig, A. G., Dieruf, W. (1966) 'The hyperactive child syndrome.' *American Journal of Orthopsychiatry,* **36,** 861.

Stores, G. (1973) 'Studies of attention and seizure disorders.' *Developmental Medicine and Child Neurology,* **15,** 376.

Strauss, A. A., Kephart, N. C. (1940) 'Behavior differences in mentally retarded children measured by a new behavior rating scale.' *American Journal of Psychiatry,* **96,** 1117.

—— Lehtinen, L. E. (1947) *Psychopathology and Education of the Brain-Injured Child,* vol. I. New York: Grune and Stratton.

Strecker, E. A., Ebaugh, F. G. (1924) 'Neuropsychiatric sequelae of cerebral trauma in children.' *Archives of Neurology and Psychiatry,* **12,** 443.

Strother, C. R. (1973) 'Minimal cerebral dysfunction: a historical overview.' *Annals of the New York Academy of Science,* **205,**

Sykes, D. H., Douglas, V. I., Morgenstern, G. (1973) 'Sustained attention in hyperactive children.' *Journal of Child Psychology and Psychiatry,* **14,** 213.

Thompson, C. I., Schwartzbaum, J. S., Harlow, H. F. (1969) 'Development of social fear after amygdalectomy in infant rhesus monkeys.' *Physiology and Behaviour,* **4,** 249.

Tiedeman, D. (1787) *Beobachtungen ueber die Entwicklung der Seelenfahrigkeiten bei Kindern.* Altenburg: Bonde.

Touwen, B. C. L. (1971) 'Neurological follow-up of infants born after obstetrical complications.' *In* Stoelinga, G. B., van der Werff ten Bosch, J. J. (Eds.) *Normal and Abnormal Development of Brain and Behaviour.* Leiden: University Press.

—— (1972) 'The relationship between neonatal and follow-up findings.' *In* Saling, E., Schutte, F. J. (Eds.) *Perinatal Medizin.* II. Stuttgart: Thieme.

—— Kalverboer, A. F. (1973) 'Neurologic and behavioural assessment of children with "Minimal Brain Dysfunction".' *In* Walzer, S., Wolff, P. (Eds.) *Minimal Cerebral Dysfunction in Children. Seminars in Psychiatry,* **5,** 79.

—— Prechtl, H. F. R. (1970) *The Neurological Examination of the Child with Minor Nervous Dysfunction.* Clinics in Developmental Medicine, no. 38. London: S.I.M.P./Heinemann.

Tulder, J. J. M. van (1962) *Sociale stijging en daling in Nederland,* III. Leiden: Stenfert-Kroeze.

Tulkin, S. R., Kagan, J. (1972) 'Mother-child interaction in the first year of life.' *Child Development,* **43,** 31.

133

Underwood, B. J. (1957) *Psychological Research*. New York: Appleton-Century-Crofts.

Vinogradova, O. S. (1961) 'The orientation reaction and its neurophysiological mechanics.' *Semya i Shkola,*

Waddington, C. H. (1971) 'Concepts of development.' *In* Tobach, E., Aronson, L. R., Shaw, E. (Eds.) *The Biopsychology of Development*. New York: Academic Press.

Walzer, S., Richmond, J. B. (1973) 'The epidemiology of learning disorders.' *Pediatric Clinics of North America,* **20,** 549.

Wedell, K. (1973) *Learning and Perceptuo-Motor Disabilities in Children*. London: John Wiley.

Wender, P. H. (1971) *Minimal Brain Dysfunction in Children*. New York: Wiley-Interscience.

Werry, J. S. (1968) 'Studies on the hyperactive child. IV. An empirical analysis of the minimal brain dysfunction syndrome.' *Archives of General Psychiatry,* **19,** 9.

—— (1972) 'Organic factors in childhood psychopathology.' *In* Quay, H. C., Werry, J. S. (Eds.) *Psychopathological Disorders in Childhood*. New York: Wiley.

Windle, W. F. (1969) 'Asphyxial brain damage at birth, with reference to minimally affected child.' *In Perinatal Factors Affecting Human Development*. Proceedings of the Special Session, 8th Meeting PAHO Advisory Committee on Medical Research, Scientific Publication, no. 185.

Wolff, P. H., Hurwitz, I. (1966) 'The choreiform syndrome.' *Developmental Medicine and Child Neurology,* **8,** 160.

—— —— (1973) 'Functional implications of the minimal brain damage syndrome.' *In* Walzer, S., Wolff, P. (Eds.) *Minimal Cerebral Dysfunction in Children. Seminars in Psychiatry,* **5,** 105.

Wylick, M. van (1936) *Die Welt des Kindes ist seiner Darstellung*. Vienna.

Zimet, C. N., Fishman, D. B. (1970) 'Psychological deficit in schizophrenia and brain damage.' *Annual Review of Psychology,* **21,** 113.